UNLOCKING REVELATION

BY DR. STAFFORD NORTH

21ST CENTURY CHRISTIAN
2809 12TH AVENUE SOUTH
NASHVILLE, TN 37204

>   Library of Congress Cataloging-in-Publication Data
>
> North, Stafford, 1930-
>   Unlocking Revelation / by Stafford North.
>   p. cm.
>   ISBN 0-89098-279-1 (pbk.)
>   1. Bible. N.T. Revelation--Commentaries. I. Title.
> BS2825.53.N67 2003
> 228'.07--dc22
>   2003019375

TABLE OF CONTENTS

INTRODUCTION

In 1974, I was asked to preach a series of sermons the following year at my home congregation, now the Memorial Road Church of Christ in Oklahoma City. After considerable thought and prayer about the topic for that series, I selected the book of Revelation. Up to that point in time, I had some ideas about the book and had taught Sunday morning Bible classes on it. With several months to prepare for the series, which was to be in September of 1975, I read something every day about Revelation—from the text, from commentaries, and from other sources.

From this intense study, I changed a number of the views I previously held about the message of the book and came to agree with what is now the most widely held position about its meaning among those not following the pre-millennial view. Some of the authors holding the view with which I generally agree are Ray Summers in *Worthy is the Lamb*, J. W. Roberts in *The Revelation to John*, and Homer Hailey in *Revelation: an Introduction and Commentary*. Other writers holding similar views are Jim McGuiggan, Raymond Kelcy, William Barclay, Henry B. Swete, Edward McDowell, Robert Mounce, John Stott, C. B. Caird, and many others.

These do not agree on all points nor does my view represent all of them. But we would all agree on the general thrust of the message.

Also during this time of study, I gave thought to the best way to present the message of Revelation to people in the pew. I decided to use an overhead projector (now PowerPoint) to project the points of the outline with accompanying Scriptures and, concurrently, to show flannel figures of the symbols on a 4' x 8' flannel board. Since the book has such a strong visual element, I wanted the sermons to be visual as well. I also sought to organize the lessons in ways that would make them easily grasped.

One element of the plan was to use an introductory lesson to review the five most common approaches to Revelation and then to follow these with seven major "keys" Revelation provides about itself. These keys allow us to make a decision about which of the five approaches is most in harmony with the book itself. Once this decision is made, it is not necessary to present what each of the five approaches believes about each symbol in the book. Rather, having made the decision early on as to which of the views is most likely the correct one, we can follow only that view through the book. This approach is much less confusing to the typical listener.

So, having gone through this process of preparation, I delivered a series of six sermons on the book of Revelation. The response was a strong approval about the clarity of the approach. Other opportunities to present the lessons in other churches developed rather quickly. Now, over twenty-five years later, I have given this series some two hundred times in everything from a university course to a one-lesson summation. It has been given in states from Hawaii to New England and in other nations: Nigeria, India, Brazil, England, and Poland. Many have said: "I have studied Revelation before, but it never really made sense for me until now." The visuals and the organization of the study have helped to make this to be true.

I have previously prepared a student workbook with a teacher's manual for a class study of thirteen lessons in Revelation and have written a book, *Armageddon Again?*, seeking to refute the pre-millennial view. In addition I have put a teacher's guide to Revelation on an internet site called www.eBibleStudy.org. Thousands of audio tapes and videotapes of the lessons have been sold. I have never before, however, collected the lessons in full written form. This book does that.

These six sermons, in a somewhat expanded form, make an interesting way to present the story of Revelation. The sermon style allows the message to be personal and informal. It also keeps the big picture in view. The sermons seek to look at Revelation in the way those who first received the book might have seen it. This is, after all, the way the book says it was to be used. Revelation 1:3 promises a blessing to the one who reads (aloud) and on those who hear and obey the book. So Christ wanted John to write down what he saw and heard and send it to the seven churches named. Then someone in the congregation would read the book aloud to the church. Imagine going to church sixty years after Jesus' death and having someone stand up and say, "I am going to read to you this morning, a letter we have just received from Jesus."

We need to study first, then, "What would the book have meant to those who first received it as they heard it being read to them?" They would not have given much attention to those small details about which some make such big points. They would have seen the big picture. They may have had inspired prophets to help them interpret it, but obviously there was a major message Jesus embedded in the book which He intended Christians to get. Like other writings addressed specifically to a particular situation, 1 Corinthians for example, Revelation, of course, has both a message for those who first received it and an application of that message which the Holy Spirit intended for us today.

So we shall share this journey through Revelation. Lesson 1 of the book introduces "seven keys" to give us direction. Lesson 2 reviews the first three chapters of Revelation, which include John's introduction and the letters to the seven churches of Asia to whom the book was originally sent. Lesson 3 presents an overview of Revelation 4 through 11 which, for reasons we shall give later, we call "Act 1" of the drama. Lesson 4 reviews Revelation 12 through 19, the major portion of "Act 2," and a part which completes the major story line of the book. Lesson 5 studies Revelation 20. This chapter gets a whole lesson both because it has been the source of many different views and because of its great practical value for us today. Lesson 6 considers Revelation 21 and 22, an opportunity to see the conclusion of the book and to get a wonderful message of hope.

The style of this book will be much as the sermons are preached. Some of the visuals used with the sermons are shown to help you visualize some of the symbols in the book. Thanks to my daughter-in-law, Beverly North, who drew these for me. Also thanks to my wife, Jo Anne, who has encouraged me in this work, provided suggestions, and who has sat through these sermons many, many times.

It will be good to read an entire chapter at one sitting, just as you would hear all of a sermon at once. And the more quickly you can read the next chapter the better. Especially look to receive the blessing Christ promises for those who "hear and obey" the book.

I hope this book will help you unlock Revelation.

LESSON 1
SEVEN KEYS THAT UNLOCK THE BOOK OF REVELATION

Just the thought of reading the Book of Revelation scares lots of people. They know it has dragons and beasts and falling stars, but they have no idea what to make of it. Some even wonder why such a book is included among the books of Scripture. Yet, Revelation 1:3 says, "Blessed is he who reads and those who hear the words of the prophecy, and heed the things which are written in it, for the time is near." God has a blessing for those who read (aloud) this book and those who hear (when it is read) and those who obey what it says. Why would God offer such a blessing if there were no chance to understand what the book means?

There is great potential value in studying the book of Revelation so we can find the message Christ wanted His churches to have. In these six lessons, we will seek to explore what the book meant to those Christians who first received it and then find from that what Christ wants us to learn for our time. Since there is so much misinformation about Revelation, we will also look at some of those views we should reject.

FIVE COMMON VIEWS OF REVELATION

Let's begin with a review the five most common interpretations of Revelation. Then we will look at seven important points the book makes about itself. Understanding these seven key points will enable us to choose from the five most popular approaches the one most in harmony with what Revelation says about itself. *These seven points, then, become keys by which we can unlock the book of Revelation.*

So we begin. If all those who write books on Revelation and who speak about it on television and radio were arranged according to their views of what Revelation means, they would fit generally into five groups. Not all in each group would agree with each other on everything and a few might not feel comfortable in any of the groups, but in general we may say that there are five common views about what Revelation means. We'll review the basics of each of these views and then take an overview of key points in the book. This will enable us to decide which of the five views is most in harmony with what the book says about itself.

The Fall of Rome. The first of the five views is that the book of Revelation was written to Christians late in the first century to deal with the coming persecution by the Roman Empire. This view holds that Christianity was about to undergo a serious threat because the Roman Empire would seek to persecute it out of existence. To encourage Christians during this difficult time, Christ sends the book of Revelation to let them know in advance about their coming trial and to promise them He will eventually bring the persecuting Empire down to defeat. Representative commentaries for this view are J. W. Roberts, *The Revelation to John* and Homer Hailey, *Commentary on Revelation.*

The Destruction of Jerusalem. The second of the common views is that the book of Revelation is primarily a message about the coming destruction of Jerusalem. According to this view, the book of Revelation was written about 65 A.D., just before Jerusalem's fall in 70

A.D. This view says the book was written to warn Christians in Jerusalem about the Roman army that was coming to destroy the Jewish capital city. After all, they say, Jesus had prophesied about this in Matthew 24, and this destruction would be a very important event in the history of Christianity. This view suggests, then, that the terrible plagues and events foretold in Revelation will be happening to those in the city of Jerusalem and sees the harlot of Revelation 17 as representing the city of Jerusalem. A commentary supporting this view is Foy E. Wallace, *The Book of Revelation.*

Foretells World History. The third of the common views is that the book of Revelation foretells major events in world history between the first and second comings of Christ. According to this view, Revelation gives a glimpse in advance of certain Roman emperors, of Mohammed, of the Turks, of the Roman Catholic Church, of war between France and England, of John Calvin and Martin Luther. This view says the major political and religious events of the Christian era are outlined in this book. Much of the focus of this view is about the Roman Catholic Church which, according to this view, is pictured as both the second beast of Revelation 13 and the harlot of Revelation 17. Commentaries presenting this view are John T. Hinds, *Revelation*, and Albert Barnes, *Notes on the New Testament.*

Principles. The fourth view may be called the "principles view" or, maybe, "the philosophical view," or the "repeating cycle" view. To those holding this approach, the book of Revelation is not about partic- ular nations, cities, or people at all, as the first three approaches suggest. This plan, rather, suggests that Revelation presents a certain sequence of events that repeats itself over and over throughout the ages. This cycle is that Jesus is proclaimed (rides forth on the white horse) and wherever He goes, political and religious persecution follow. This view says this happened during the Roman days, but that the Roman persecution was not the primary focus of the book. The cycle, they say, can fit equally well any other time of proclamation and persecution. So this view is called the "principles" view because it presents certain principles or a philosophy of history that repeat throughout the ages. Some, but not all who hold this view, believe the story of events between the first coming and second coming of Christ is told seven times in the book of Revelation. Thus, Christ's coming would be portrayed seven times in the book. Burton Coffman's commentary on Revelation and W. Hendriksen's *More Than Conquerors* take this view.

Future Time. The fifth of the common approaches, and one we hear about more than any other, may be called the future time view. This is, for example, the view promoted in the popular "Left Behind" series of novels. Those who approach this way say that nearly all of the events described in Revelation are still to come. Maybe we are now living, they say, in chapter three and all the rest is still future. This view says there will soon come a moment in time when all living Christians will be taken away and all dead Christians will be raised from the dead. This moment is called "the rapture." The "raptured" go into heaven for seven years while on earth the Jewish temple is rebuilt and there is war over Israel. At the height of this war, the battle of Armageddon will involve 300,000,000 soldiers in Israel. (In Operation Iraqi Freedom, the coalition forces only numbered about 300,000, so there will be a hundred times as many in this battle, they say.) In the midst of this, Jesus will return and put down the fighting and establish His own kingdom over the world. He will reign in Jerusalem for a thousand years with the raptured, who return to earth with Him, and also with the Old Testament good people who are raised when He returns, and with those in their mortal bodies who have served him on earth during the seven years of tribulation. At the end of the thousand years of bliss on earth comes the end of time, which brings a third resurrection, the resurrection of the wicked. Now comes the judgment of the wicked (Revelation 20) and the separation into heaven and hell. Those who hold this view think the book of Revelation contains much of this story but also draw some of it from other places in the Bible. Hal Lindsey's *There's a New World Coming* and Robert Shank's *Until* present this view.

So, five common views, each claiming to be the intended meaning of the book of Revelation. Which shall we take? The best way to answer this question is first to learn some things the book of Revelation says about itself. So let's turn to seven key points about the book, from the book.

SEVEN KEYS TO UNDERSTANDING
THE BOOK OF REVELATION

Revelation is Written in Symbols. The first key the book of Revelation gives about itself is that it's contents are clearly different from most other books in the Bible. Just scanning through the book we see a seven-headed dragon, a seven-headed beast with ten horns, a lamb with seven horns and seven eyes, seas turning to blood, horses with fire and smoke coming out of their mouths, a woman who stands on the moon, a city in the shape of a cube that is 1,500 miles in each direction, and many more. Obviously we are not reading a book like Colossians. Someone called Revelation God's comic book.

So, how do we approach such a book? Should we think Revelation wants us to believe there is actually a dragon large enough to draw a third of the stars out of the sky, or is this a figure of speech? The Bible certainly does use figurative language in many places. Jesus, for example, says He is the "bread of life," but we know He's not literal bread. He says He is the "water of life," but we know He's not literal water. These are figures He uses to teach us that He's as essential to our spiritual life as bread and water are to our physical life. So, figures of speech work like this:

The top hand represents "what it says" while the bottom hand represents "what it means." So Jesus says "bread of life" (top hand) but He means He's as essential to us spiritually as bread is physically (bottom hand). This is the way with figures. What it says—What it means.

But how do we know whether to take something literally or figuratively? An important question, but one we deal with many times a day and have little trouble. If I should say to you, for example, "I'm burning up," what would you think? Would you call the fire department? No, you'd just know I mean that I'm warmer than I want to be. If, on the other hand, I should say "I'm freezing to death," you wouldn't call the undertaker. You'd know I just mean I'm cooler than I want to be.

The "rule of thumb" we use in every day language is that any statement that, on its face, is absurd or extreme if taken literally, is likely intended to be a figure of speech. The sports announcer, for example, may say a basketball player is "quick as lightning," or that a tight end is "like a bullet" running down the sidelines. We immediately know how to switch from the literal to the figurative. So we come to Revelation with its long list of characters and events that appear absurd or extreme if taken literally, and we take them figuratively.

Scholars speak of Revelation as being of a particular "genre," meaning a particular type of literature. Some books of the Bible are history, some are law, some are poetry, some are epistles. Revelation belongs in the type called "apocalypse." In fact, that is really the second word in the first verse of the book, "apocalypse" often translated "revelation." When we match Revelation against the characteristics of this type of literature, it is clear that Christ used this genre to convey His message. Apocalyptic literature is presented as a vision; it uses animals and numbers in figurative ways, it predicts historical events, and usually gives hope in a time of hardship. As we shall see, Revelation fits all of these characteristics.

So, when we come to the book of Revelation, we will take some things literally because there really was an island named Patmos and cities named Ephesus and Pergamum. But since most of the book uses horses, dragons, lambs, beasts, locusts, rivers of blood, the sun going dark, women standing on the moon, and a city in the shape of a cube, we will wear our "figurative hat" on most of the time.

As we seek to decide, then, which view of Revelation to take, we will choose one that fits this key: *The book of Revelation makes heavy use of symbols.*

Revelation Will "Shortly Come to Pass." The second key to Revelation is that it's written about events that will "shortly come to pass." The book provides its own time-frame for *when* its events will happen. The very first verse of the very first chapter says it will be about "things that must shortly come to pass." Notice these other verses which speak about the time-frame of the book: 1:3—"the time is at hand"; 3:11—"I come quickly"; 22:6—"things which must shortly come to pass"; 22:7—"I come quickly"; 22:10—"seal not up the prophecy of this book; for the time is at hand"; 22:12—"I come quickly"; 22:20—"I come quickly." What message, do you suppose, did those first hearing it get from such language? Obviously the writer intends to emphasize that the book is primarily about events that will begin quickly after the book is delivered and will play out in a relatively short time frame.

In the verses where Jesus says "I come quickly," He clearly is not speaking of His second coming. If He were, He would have been mistaken, for His second coming did not happen soon after the book was written. Rather, He was speaking of His coming to carry out the promises and predictions He makes in this book. A ruler, for example, may be said to "come" to carry out some action without actually being physically present. One might say, for example, that President George W. Bush went to Iraq and defeated Saddam Hussein, but he did not go there in person. The Bible speaks of God's "coming" to carry out His predictions. When Isaiah pictures a destruction in Egypt, for example, he says, "the Lord rides on a swift cloud and is coming to Egypt" (Isaiah 19:1). So the Lord will "come" to carry out a promised destruction but this does not mean a physical coming of God. God came, in this case, through an Assyrian ruler who carried out the prophesied destruction on Egypt. So, when Christ promises to "come quickly" in Revelation, He does not mean that His second coming will be soon. Rather, He means He will "come quickly" to carry out the promises and threats He makes in Revelation.

We must put ourselves in the place of those who first received the book—Christians living in Ephesus and Pergamum and Thyatira and Laodicea. These Christians, living in the Roman province of Asia Minor during the last days of the first century, would have understood these verses to mean that this message is about things that would take place in their day and in the time immediately following. Certainly the words "soon" and "quickly" are intended to give an immediacy to the message for those who first received it. To think that a gap of two thousand years would take place before the book's main thrust is carried out is to miss the intent of many passages in the book.

The second key, then, is recognizing the time-table the book of Revelation gives for itself. It contains a message about something to begin immediately after the book is revealed to early Christians and the events it describes will play out within a short period of time. As we study the book, it will be clear that the story began at the time the book was delivered and played out in the years immediately following. The message to early Christians clearly was, *"Look for these things to begin happening soon."*

Revelation is Given to Comfort Persecuted Christians. The third key to understanding Revelation the book itself gives is that its underlying theme is the persecution of the church. Someone has said "the blood of Christians is on every page." By this they meant that whatever page of the book you choose, something on that page will speak about the persecution of Christians. To see that persecution is a pervasive theme of the book, look at just a few of the passages on that topic. In 1:9, John says to other Christians, "I am a partaker with you in the tribulation." So both John, who was exiled on the Island of Patmos for his faith, and the Christians to whom he is writing, are involved in "tribulation" for their faith. Chapters 2 and 3 contain seven letters Christ dictates to seven churches. In five of the seven letters, He mentions persecution. In addition, look at Revelation 6:9-11, the most significant passage in the whole book in disclosing the meaning of Revelation. Here the souls of those who have been beheaded for their testimony, later in 12:17 and 20:4 called "the testimony of Jesus," shout a question: "How long, O Master, Holy and True, do you not judge and avenge our blood on those who are on the earth?" They have been martyred for the cause of Christ and want to know how long before those who killed them will be brought to justice. God answers that He will not take this action immediately, but will, rather, allow time for more of their brothers to be killed as they have been. So, there *has been persecution* of Christians and, before God brings it to an end and the persecutor to justice, there *will be more persecution.* As the story of Revelation unfolds, we'll see how God responds to this cry of the martyrs, first to wait a while, and then to do just as they have asked.

Other verses further demonstrating the underlying theme of persecution are found in 7:14, where a great host in heaven are said to have come out of the great tribulation, the death of the two witnesses in chapter 11, the plan of the dragon to persecute those who hold the testimony of Jesus in chapter 12, the beast making war on the saints in 13:7, the second beast killing those who will not worship the beast in 13:15, in 17:6 the harlot has spilled the blood of the saints, in 18:24 the blood of Christians is found in Babylon, and in 20:4 those who were beheaded for the testimony of Jesus are seen reigning with Christ.

Surely there can be no doubt that, with these and many other verses telling of the persecution of Christians, something relating to persecution lies at the heart of the message of the book. And, if persecution is the theme, there also can be no doubt that the message is intended as one of comfort and encouragement to those who will be subjected to this persecution. Christ would not send a book to Christians so full of references to persecution about to come upon them and not accompany that news with a message to help. You don't visit someone in the hospital with pneumonia and talk of all those who died of this disease; you provide, rather, a message of comfort.

Revelation, then, is a book about the persecution of Christians, and those who first received the book were about to undergo the worst persecution the church has ever faced. These Christians needed to know not only what was coming, but how God was eventually going to settle the outcome. This message, although it contained the bad news of the persecution, contained the good news of how God would punish the persecutor and honor the faithful.

The third key, then, is that *the message of Revelation is to comfort persecuted Christians.*

Revelation Identifies the Dragon and Two Beasts. As we said earlier, the book of Revelation makes use of symbols to communicate its message. Some of these symbols portray major characters in the story of the book. If we can correctly identify who these major characters are, we will have discovered a very important key to understanding the book. Three of these major players appear as a dragon and two beasts. Let's see if the book will tell us who these are.

The dragon. The dragon is introduced in Revelation 12 and is seen through the remainder of the book. The book pictures him as red, with seven heads and ten horns and seven crowns. Such a description certainly suggests power and rulership of some kind. With his tail, he sweeps a third of the stars from the sky, indicating not only power but that this is not just any large animal. He persecutes a woman and her child and he brings up two beasts to be his helpers in persecuting God's people. Later he is bound in the abyss for a thousand years and then is thrown into the Lake of Fire. We really are not left in doubt about the identity of the dragon. Revelation 12:9 and 20:2 state plainly that the dragon is "the old serpent who is called 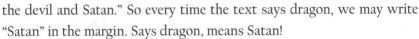 the devil and Satan." So every time the text says dragon, we may write "Satan" in the margin. Says dragon, means Satan!

The first beast. Identifying the first beast may be the most important identification in the book. That the dragon means Satan seems abundantly clear since two verses state that point in very plain language. Since the beast plays such a crucial role in the story, it is also very important that his identity be known. A misread on this one could lead us in a wrong direction. While no single verse declares who he is in specific terms, there are plenty of clues, and there is agreement, even among many who follow different approaches, as to who he is. Look at this representation of the beast. Let's study the clues and see if we can make a firm identification.

In the last verse of chapter 12, the dragon (Satan) goes to make war on those who keep God's commands and who hold the testimony of Jesus. In the very next verse, 13:1, John sees a fierce red beast coming up out of the water. And since in 13:7 the beast is said to "make war with the saints," it is clear that Satan brings up the beast as his agent to persecute Christians. So the first mark of identity is that the beast is a major persecutor of Christians.

As this beast comes into view, he is seen to have ten horns spread on seven heads and on each horn is a crown. His body is like a leopard, his mouth like a lion, and his paws like a bear. So, he is made of parts from three animals—a lion, a bear, and a leopard—and has ten horns. Such a description will remind those who know the Old Testament of

the prophecy in Daniel 7 where there are four beasts—a lion, a bear, a leopard, and a beast with ten horns. Surely some connection is intended. In Daniel's prophecy, the four animals each represent a major world empire: the lion is Babylon, the bear depicts the Medes and Persians; the leopard stands for the fast moving Grecian Empire of Alexander the Great; and the fourth, with the ten horns, represents the Roman Empire. It is interesting to note that the same four empires are represented by the parts of the image in Nebuchadnezzar's dream in Daniel 2. So by using the imagery of empires in Daniel 7, John clearly is suggesting that this beast, like those in Daniel, represents a major world power. John's beast, of course, has a particular relationship to Daniel's fourth beast, the Roman Empire, because they both are pictured with ten horns. Since each empire in Daniel was composed of much of the same territory as the preceding ones, it's not unusual that the fourth one is pictured as being made up of parts of the previous three.

So the first two clues would suggest that this beast is the Roman Empire which persecuted Christians. But do the other clues about this beast in Revelation agree that it represents the Roman Empire? Let's see.

In Revelation 13:6-7 we get more important clues. Here the beast is given four qualities: (1) he blasphemes God; (2) he makes war on the saints; (3) he reigns over every tribe, people, language and nation, and (4) the inhabitants of the earth worship the beast. So the beast stands for a worldwide empire with a religion that deifies its own leaders to become objects of worship, and it's an empire that opposes God and persecutes Christians. Our identification of the beast must match these characteristics.

Revelation 17:9-10 gives additional clues for the identity of the beast. Here we are told that each of the seven heads represents a king. John says that five of the seven kings have already reigned, *one is reigning at the time of his writing*, and another is yet to come. Thus the beast exists at the time John is writing, for he says one of the kings "is" and another is yet to come. So the heads of this beast represent kings and one is in power as John writes the book. These verses also tell us that the seven heads not only stand for seven kings, but they also represent seven hills. What would have come to the minds of those Christians who first received Revelation at the mention of seven hills?

Now let's think like first-century Christians about these clues. What would have come to their minds when they thought of a beast with the following characteristics? It is a major world power, ruling over the world. Its leaders are the objects of worship and, since one of its kings is in power when John writes, it represents the major world power during their day. They would also understand that the beast represents the major persecutor of Christians of their time, that he was connected with seven hills, and that he was portrayed in Daniel as a beast with ten horns. What would these clues have brought to their minds? Clearly there can be but one entity that fits all these clues: the Roman Empire. This world-wide empire that ruled during John's day was the fourth beast of Daniel, its emperors were worshipped, its capital city, Rome, was built on seven hills, and it was a strong persecutor of Christians. So, early Christians would have known that whenever the text refers to this first beast, it means Roman Empire. Says beast, means Roman Empire!

Second beast. The dragon (Satan) also brings up a second beast in Revelation 13. The only description of this beast is that he has two horns like a lamb.

What would early Christians have made of this animal? Here are the clues. He arises in chapter 13 with the first beast (the Roman Empire) and goes down to defeat with the first beast in chapter 19. So this beast exists concurrently with the first beast—they come up together and fall together. This second beast is also said to exercise his authority "in the sight" of the first beast. This precludes identifying the second beast as something that continues *after* the first beast is gone for the two exist and work together. In addition, the second beast speaks like a dragon and, thus, is the tool of Satan. The second beast is presented as having only one mission—to set up images or statues of the heads of the beast (Roman emperors) and force people to worship them. To do this, he deceives with false miracles, uses economic pressure, and even kills those who refuse to worship the beast.

So, how would early Christians have identified this second beast whose sole purpose is to force people to worship the emperors of the Roman Empire? To the first century mind, this picture would have been clear. Beginning particularly during the reign of the Roman Emperor Domitian, 81-96 AD, emperor worship became a major force in Roman life. A strong cult of emperor worship developed, built images and even erected large, elaborate temples to the Roman Emperors where they were to be worshipped. People were required to take a pinch of incense and burn it on the altar to an emperor and confess "Caesar is Lord." Refusing to take this pledge was considered an act of treason. So when Christians refused to participate in this worship to emperors, they became the enemies of the state and this, in turn, became the basis of intense persecution. To those in the area of the seven churches of Asia, to whom Revelation was originally addressed, there would have been no difficulty in knowing who this second beast was: The Cult of Emperor Worship. In Ephesus, for example, right next to the major downtown market area, there was a huge temple to three Roman Emperors: Vespasian, Titus, and Domitian.

So the dragon is Satan, the first beast is the Roman Empire and the second beast is the Cult of Emperor Worship.

Revelation Identifies the Harlot Who is Babylon. The book of Revelation also has a figure in the story-line called a harlot or prostitute. She is introduced in Revelation 17 and from that chapter we learn these things about her. She is a "great city" (v. 18), she commits fornication with kings (v. 2), she rides upon or rules over the first beast (vs. 3, 7), she is dressed luxuriously in purple and scarlet and wears precious jewels (v. 4), and she holds in her hand a cup filled with the blood of the saints and, having drunk so much of their blood, she is intoxicated. So, the harlot is a city who rules over the beast (Roman Empire), who leads the kings of the world in immorality, is rich and luxurious, and leads in the persecution of Christians.

Early Christians would certainly have recognized this city as the City of Rome. As further confirmation of this identification, she wears a headband with this inscription: "Mystery, Babylon the Great, The Mother of Harlots, and of the Abominations of the Earth." Her name, then, is "Babylon." Since ancient Babylon was the capital city of a great world empire that persecuted God's people, this is an appropriate name for the capital city of the Roman Empire, also a persecutor of God's people. Some in the first century, even referred to Rome as Babylon. *So the harlot named Babylon is the city of Rome.*

Just another word about the harlot. Another indication that she represents the city of Rome is the fact that a popular coin in circulation in Asia Minor at the time Revelation was written pictures Rome as a beautiful woman, luxuriously arrayed. This coin, one of which is at the British Museum, shows that depicting Rome as an elegant woman would have been familiar to the people of that day.

Revelation Identifies the 1260 Days. There is a time period mentioned five times in the book of Revelation, all in chapters 11, 12, and 13. Twice it is called 1260 days, twice 42 months, and once three and a half years (time, times, and half a time). All of these suggest a period of the same length for 1260 days divided by 30 would be 42 months and 42 months divided by 12 would be three and a half years. What happens during this period? In 11:2 Gentiles are said to tread over the holy city for 42 months; in 11:3 and 7, the two witnesses (God's people) are said to testify for 1260 days while under attack and at the end of which period they are killed in the city of the beast; in 12:6 a woman, precious to God, is nourished and protected from Satan for 1260 days; in 12:14 God nourishes the woman for a time, times, and half a time to protect her from Satan; and in 13:7 the beast will make war with the saints for 42 months. Note what all of these time periods have in common! Whether spoken of in days, months, or years, the activity mentioned is always an attack on what God considers precious, particularly His saints. In two of the events Satan is said to be the attacker and in three the beast (Roman Empire) is the attacker. So, the 1260 days would be a time of persecution of God's people, and, in particular, an attack directed by Satan using the Roman Empire.

Since the Roman Empire did persecute Christians from about 90 AD to about 300 AD, this period of time would be what is represented by the 1260 days. Remember that in Revelation, not only are animals and other objects to be taken figuratively, but time periods are also figurative. We would not expect, then, that the 1260 days would be an actual three and a half years but a time period representing a period in which some major event is going to take place. *So, the 1260 days represents the period of time during which the Roman Empire will persecute the church.*

Revelation Identifies the Kingdom. The book of Revelation speaks of a "kingdom" and gives us information about it that is useful in understanding the book. Since some teach that the kingdom of God in Revelation is a reign of Christ on earth, it will be helpful, even at this early point in our study, to see how the book describes the kingdom of which it speaks. In Revelation 1:6, John says Christ "made us to be a kingdom and priests to serve his God." We learn much from this simple phrase. John speaks of the kingdom as *in existence* at his time—Christ has already "made," past tense, a kingdom. So John and those early Christians to whom he wrote were already in the kingdom. And the kingdom is one whose citizens are priests—thus it is a spiritual kingdom and not one reigning over earthly territory.

Just three verses later, in verse 9, John says that he and those to whom he is writing are partakers or companions "in the kingdom." Again, John speaks of the kingdom as existing in his day and both he and the Christians to whom he writes are in it. In chapter 5, verses 9 and 10, the kingdom is mentioned again. Here Christ is being extolled as worthy because he has "purchased men for God from every tribe and language and people and nation." He has already "made them to be a kingdom." So by the time of the writing of this book, Christ has already established His kingdom and people from all nations are in it. This verse, like 1:6 also speaks of the citizens of the kingdom as priests, again emphasizing the spiritual nature of the kingdom. This passage adds that these will "reign on the earth." The word "on" here would better be translated "over." Even though these people will be persecuted, they will eventually triumph, as shown by the promise they will some day reign over, or be victorious over, those who have persecuted them. That is really the major theme of Revelation. While there will be a time of suffering for Christians, their faithfulness will eventually win the day and they will be victorious.

These thoughts about the kingdom are in harmony with what Jesus said about His kingdom as He spoke with Pilate. In John 18:33-36, Pilate asked Jesus if He were a king. Jesus replied, "My kingdom is not of this world. . . . My kingdom is from another place." So, by the description in Revelation and by Jesus' own words, we should not think of Jesus' kingdom as an earthly kingdom like the kingdoms of this world. Rather, it is a spiritual kingdom and early Christians were in it.

A REVIEW OF THE FIVE APPROACHES

So, which of the five approaches we introduced earlier is most likely to be the message God was giving the early Christians who first received the book? And which would, then, be the approach from which God still wants us to learn today? Let's make a brief comparison.

The "Future Time" View. Our study would *not* support the "futurist" view as the one early Christians would have drawn from Revelation. The book says its scenario will occur "soon," but this approach suggests that the major thrust of the book has not happened even after two thousand years. The book identifies the beast as the Roman Empire existing at the time the book was written. Those holding the future time view typically agree that the beast represents the Roman Empire, but they say it is a "revived" Roman Empire that will come back, arising out of today's European Common Market. A modern day group of nations, however, cannot match the picture Revelation gives of its beast.

This future time view, which includes a modern war over the middle east, would have offered no appropriate message to comfort the Christians of Ephesus or Smyrna or Thyatira who were about to undergo the terrible Roman persecution. Revelation is clearly focused on the immediate threat to Christianity about which Christ wants both to warn and to comfort. Telling these people about a war to take place two thousand years after their time would have been of little benefit to them.

The "futurist" view also takes most of the "pictures" in Revelation as literal rather than symbolic. The "locusts" John saw, they say, really are modern day helicopters but since John didn't have "helicopter" in his vocabulary, he just used the word locust. And, they say, the sea turning to blood was John's way of describing modern problems of pollution. And the horses with fire and smoke coming out of their mouths are modern day tanks. Such a view makes most of the book to be literal rather than figurative, and this is not its intent.

The future view makes the first beast to be "the Roman anti-christ" who will come just before the end of the world, and makes the second beast to be "the Jewish anti-christ" who will come at the same time. Early Christians would have been familiar with John's discussion of "anti-christ" in which he says many anti-christs will come in the first century denying the divinity of Christ (1 John 2:18, 22). They certainly would not, therefore, have thought of the beasts as representing one or two anti-christs coming near the end of time. If, then, we start our interpretation by asking what the message would have meant to those who first received it, this view of the beasts would not have been it.

This "futurist" approach, moreover, makes the kingdom to be a physical, earthly power yet to be established, while Revelation speaks of the kingdom as a spiritual reign then going on and of which John and the early Christians were already a part. And this view makes the 1260 days a time of war in Israel just before Christ's second coming, certainly not what we have seen as the way Revelation describes this period as a time of persecution of Christians who refuse to worship the emperor. As we move through the book of Revelation in coming lessons, we will learn more about what all these things represent and will have much more to say about this "futurist" approach, but even at the outset, this view does not fit well with what we have learned.

The "Philosophical" View. This view proposes that the book of Revelation has a message for all times and places. And with that much of this approach I agree. Yes, there are lessons here for all of us, and in this series we will have much to say about such applications. At the same time, however, Revelation's primary audience was those who first received it toward the end of the first century and the book is deeply rooted in their time and circumstances. The book says it is primarily about what would take place "soon," but the "philosophical" approach makes it equally applicable to all times and places. The first beast is clearly the Roman Empire, but this view makes it to be any persecuting political power. The second beast clearly represents emperor worship, but this view makes it to be any false religion or philosophy opposed to Christianity. And the harlot is certainly the city of Rome, not, as this view takes her, worldly temptations for those who are Christians. This view makes the 1260 days to be the entire Christian era, which does not fit the description Revelation gives of that period. So, while this view rightly encourages us to find applications in the book for our time and place, it takes Revelation out of its original setting and primary meaning. Certainly such a view is not what first century Christians would have seen, nor is it the best view for us to take.

Foretells World History. This view suggests that Revelation predicts the history of the world between Christ's first coming and His second coming. Such a view is clearly not what early Christians would have seen in the book and so is not the best approach for us to take either. While there certainly are some predictions of historical events in the book, it does not seek to outline the religious and political history of the entire Christian era. The book says it is about what will "shortly come to pass," starting from the time of those who first received it. It is a message of comfort to these early, persecuted Christians, but sketching for them the religious and political events of the next two thousand or more years would not have given them much comfort for their coming persecution. This approach makes the first beast to be the Roman Empire, which I believe is correct. But it makes the second beast to be the Roman Catholic Church, which I believe does not fit the intent of the book. These two beasts come up together, go down together, and the second beast seeks only to get people to worship the emperors. Whatever one thinks of the Catholic church, this description does not fit it. The Catholic church did not arise until after the Roman Empire had fallen and it does not seek to force worship of Roman emperors. This view makes the 1260 days to be the "dark ages" which, again, does not fit Revelation's description of the period as a time of persecution of Christians by the beast. So, this approach does not fit well what the book of Revelation tells us about itself.

The Fall of Jerusalem. This view applies the book of Revelation to the fall of Jerusalem in 70 AD, but several things we have learned from the book do not fit this approach. While this view agrees that the beast is the Roman Empire, it makes the harlot to be Jerusalem. But Jerusalem certainly didn't rule over (sit on the back of) the Roman Empire. This view makes the 1260 days to be the period of the Roman siege of Jerusalem but that was not a "war on the saints," for most of the Christians escaped from Jerusalem before this siege began. And there are other problems with this view. It would require the book of Revelation to have been written prior to the fall of Jerusalem in 70 AD but the evidence does not support such an early date. The earliest mention of the book of Revelation outside the New Testament suggests that it was in circulation in 95 AD. Surely if it were written thirty years earlier, there would be some earlier reference to it. The descriptions of the seven churches does not match the conditions of those churches in the sixties. Then they would have been young churches, but the descriptions in Revelation suggest churches that have been in existence much longer. And there is a particular problem for this view. Why would Christ direct a message about the fall of Jerusalem to seven churches in the Roman province of Asia Minor, far removed from Jerusalem? If the fall of that city were His focus, why not write to Christians in Jerusalem about it? Christians in these Roman cities would have had little connection with Jerusalem. So, this view does not fit well with what we know about Revelation.

The Fall of Rome. This view suggests that the primary message of the book is to inform early Christians that Satan will be using the Roman Empire and the Cult of Emperor Worship to persecute the church out of existence. So the book of Revelation is Christ's way of encouraging Christians to be "faithful unto death" during this critical time. This approach certainly has much to recommend it. It takes the various characters in the book as figurative: the dragon as Satan, the beast as the Roman Empire, the second beast as the Cult of Emperor Worship, and the harlot as the city of Rome. This view fits "shortly come to pass" because the story this view presents begins immediately after the book was written, toward the end of the first century with the Roman persecution, and plays out over the following years until the final fall of Rome in 475 AD. This view, as shown in the book, focuses on persecution of the church primarily over the refusal of Christians to worship the emperor. This approach makes the 1260 days to be the symbolic time of the Roman persecution and takes the kingdom to be a spiritual one of which John and early Christians were members. In short, this view matches all of the seven keys we drew from the book itself.

While learning which basic approach to take in studying the book of Revelation does not answer all the questions about the book, *it is a very good start*. It allows us to follow this track through the book, thus not being confused by trying to keep all the tracks in mind at once. As we move through the next five lessons, then, we will give our primary attention to developing the view that Revelation is primarily a message to early Christians about the coming Roman persecution. It also includes a promise that God has not forgotten them through this time and that He will eventually bring the persecutor down to defeat.

CONCLUSION

So, from this very first lesson, we understand there are many clues to the meaning of Revelation, and, if we decipher the most basic ones first, we can know how to approach the book. A very important factor in this process is to see the book through the eyes of Christians in the first century. When we do, we will understand the general thrust of the book to be a message of encouragement and hope to those Christians who are about to undergo the most intense persecution Christ's followers have ever experienced. The book was written in a figurative "code" because to have put this message about the Roman Empire in more literal language would have only have given the Romans another reason to consider the church as a group of traitors.

From this introductory survey of Revelation, we now understand which of the five most common views to take as we proceed through the book. And, as we see the book unfold in the next five lessons, we will recognize that it was not only a book of great value to the early Christians but has many benefits for us today as well.

LESSON 2
THE SEVEN CHURCHES

REVELATION 1-3
CHAPTER 1: INTRODUCTION TO THE BOOK

Having studied some background information about Revelation in the first lesson, we come now to study the book chapter by chapter. You can have your Bible open as we go so you can look up some verses for yourself.

As Revelation begins in chapter 1, verse 1, we see the order through which the inspired message was delivered. It began in the mind of God, who gave it to Christ, who gave it to an angel, who delivered it to John. Thus, the message in Revelation is of divine origin. The verse also says this message will make known to His servants "what must soon take place." So the book is particularly to reveal to those who first received it what they needed to know about things that would happen soon.

The John who received this message and sent it to others was on the Island of Patmos "because of the word of God." Likely he was being exiled there to limit his ability to proclaim the message of Christ. Since he identifies himself only as "John," and gives no other identification, he must have been a well-known John. Most believe he was the apostle John who is known to have been in Ephesus, not far from Patmos. There are similarities in the vocabulary to John's gospel and epistles and early Christian writers speak of the author as being the apostle John.

John says he was "in the Spirit" on the Lord's Day. This would suggest he was in a worshipful mood on a Sunday, thinking on spiritual matters. Suddenly he heard behind him a loud voice, like a trumpet, which told him, "Write on a scroll what you see and send it to the churches in Ephesus, Smyrna, Pergamum, Thyatira, Sardis, Philadelphia, and Laodicea. These cities are all close together along the western edge of the Roman province of Asia Minor, now the country of Turkey. Six of them were in a quarter-circle to the north and east of Ephesus. They were all major cities with a large population, major buildings and markets, and with places to worship pagan gods.

When John turned to see who was speaking in the trumpet-like voice, he saw a human-like figure walking among seven golden lampstands. His face was shining, his hair white, and a two-edged sword was coming out of his mouth. He was clothed to the foot with a white robe and had a golden sash around his waist. His feet were like polished brass. In his right hand he held seven stars.

John was so overcome by this vision, he fell as if dead at the feet of the one he saw. We might say John was scared to death. And who wouldn't be at seeing such a person and hearing him speaking. But the figure said to John, "Do not be afraid. I am the First and the Last. I am the Living One. I was dead, and behold I am alive forever and ever! And I hold the keys of death and Hades" (1:17-18).

Are there enough clues here for us to know who is speaking? Since we are in Revelation, we expect symbolic pictures, and here we have the first one. Who only could say, "I was dead and am alive for ever and ever?" Who, in human-looking form, could say, I am the first and the last and the living one?" Who holds the keys of death and Hades? Surely only one could fit these clues: Jesus Christ. He is pictured as a human being, but He is also divine. He was dead but is alive. He was killed but is now the ruler of death and Hades. He was subject to human mistreatment but now holds power. The Word of God proceeds from His mouth.

He tells John to write what he has seen, what is now, and what will happen later. And he explains two of the elements of the vision. The seven lampstands, He says, represent the seven churches to whom He writes. What a glorious picture of a church—a lampstand. What better way to describe a congregation of God's people than as a light on a stand—sharing the message of truth, setting an example, being a light-giver to all around. Each of our congregations should seek to fulfill this image—we are light-givers to the world.

Jesus also tells John the meaning of the seven stars in His right hand. These are the "angels" of the seven churches. We have to do a little deciphering here because the word "angel" can have more than one meaning. The root meaning of angel is "messenger." The word usually speaks of those heavenly messengers who carry out God's bidding. They were created before He created the world and exist to serve Him. But the word "angel" also may refer to human beings who are messengers. In the famous passage about John the Baptist, he is called a "messenger" (angel) who will go before the face of the Messiah (Mark 1:2). Here the "angel" is John, a human messenger. So, does Jesus here mean that each church has a heavenly messenger or that each church has an earthly messenger?

To help us understand this, we should note that in chapters two and three, each of the letters to the seven churches is addressed "To the angel of the church" in a certain city. So Jesus tells John to address each letter to the "angel" of each church and, presumably, to send it to that angel. This would seem to argue for the "angels" to be those human beings who sent and received messages for the churches. Thus, each letter is addressed to the person who serves as the "corresponding secretary" for each congregation. If the letters, on the other hand, were addressed to a heavenly messenger, in what post office would John deposit the letters to send them there? It's no big deal in our understanding of the book, but it would seem that the "angels" are members of each congregation who will receive the letters and communicate them to the congregation.

CHAPTERS 2 AND 3: LETTERS TO THE SEVEN CHURCHES

We come now to chapters 2 and 3. These two chapters contain the seven letters which Jesus dictated to John and which he, in turn, is to send to the seven churches. Imagine you are sitting in the congregational meeting of the church in Ephesus one Sunday morning about 90 AD and an elder of the church solemnly rises. He says to those assembled, "We have received a letter to this church in Ephesus from Jesus, Himself. He appeared to John, who is exiled on Patmos, and told him what to write to us. Even though Jesus has been dead for sixty years, today we have a message directly from Him to our congregation." Something like that happened in all the seven churches.

Many have done wonderful studies of each of the seven letters, but our time doesn't allow us to study each of them in detail. Rather, we'll look at all the letters together by asking the question, "What themes appear as we look at all these letters together? What subjects seem to be on the heart of Jesus as He writes to His churches?" Surely if some things are mentioned in all or most of the letters, these things would be very important to Jesus. Also the recurring topics in these letters would likely be the things Jesus would say to us today if He were writing us. Indeed there are such themes and, to match the number of churches, we will discuss seven of them.

1. The first theme we notice in reading the letters is this: *Jesus knows His churches.* Expressions such as "I know your deeds," "I know your afflictions," "I know where you live," run through the letters. And the letters show clearly that Jesus did know the churches and the individuals. He mentions Antipas of Pergamum by name, He knows about the actions

of some in Thyatira and Pergamum who are teaching error, and He knows of many who are living faithfully. Jesus knows His people.

And He also knows us today. He knows us, in fact, very intimately. He knows our words, our actions, and our thoughts. He knows where we go and what we do. He knows our sorrows and our disappointments, our challenges and our victories. How do you feel when you think about how well Jesus knows you? Do you rejoice that He walks "hand in hand" with you through life's journey, or do you, like Adam and Eve, wish you could hide from God's presence. Part of Christ's all-knowing power is to know each of us, His disciples, and we need to live each day in that full realization. I hope it gives you comfort to sense His presence. But if it makes you uncomfortable to know that Jesus is constantly with you, that's a good signal you need to make some changes in your life.

2. The second theme: *Christ wants churches to guard their teaching.* In Revelation 2:2, Christ praises the Ephesian church because they have "tested" those who claimed to be apostles and found them false. They also hated the work of the Nicolaitans. While we do not know exactly what the false apostles or the Nicolaitans were teaching, it is clear that they were teaching something that did not correspond to what the Ephesians had heard from inspired teachers like Paul and possibly John himself before he was exiled. The critical point here is that the elders of the church in Ephesus were doing just as Paul had commanded when he spoke to them in Acts 20. They were being very alert about keeping false teachers from coming among the flock; they were guarding the sheep from savage wolves.

In Revelation 2:14 and 2:20, on the other hand, Jesus condemns the churches of Pergamum and Thyatira because they had not been vigilant. They had allowed people to teach that it was not a sin to commit fornication or to eat meat offered to idols. Probably these teachers had said something like this: since the human body is really meaningless, it doesn't matter if the body sins so long as the soul is not involved. Jesus, speaking through John, makes it clear that what the body does involves the mind and heart and thus, if the body does what is wrong, sin takes place. The point here is that these churches had allowed false teachers to go unchecked and Christ reproves them for that.

In Revelation 3:3, Christ urges the church in Sardis to remember what they received and to keep it. This charge sounds much like what John had written in 1 John 2:24: "See that what you have heard from the beginning remains in you. If it does, you also will remain in the Son and in the Father." Finally, in Revelation 3:8, Jesus praises the Philadelphia church for "keeping His word."

These five citations from the letters, then, reveal one of the critical issues on the heart of Jesus: you have been taught the Word of God correctly, and it is essential that you hold to this teaching and not drift away. Unfortunately the Bible story is filled with cases of God's people leaving His instruction. God teaches His people what He wants them to do, then they wander away from this message, then God sends punishment to make them think, and then they cry out in their troubles for God to remove the punishment, promising they will be better. But they only stay with God's teaching for a short time until they drift away again. Think of Adam and Eve, the Israelites as they made the golden calf in the wilderness, the Israelites in the time of the judges and kings. It is of just such a departure from what God has revealed that Paul warns in Acts 20:30 and in 1 Timothy 4:1-4 and in 2 Timothy 4:1-4. We must understand this tendency to drift away and make a determined stand not to leave God's way but to hold fast to what we have been taught from the Word. We need to learn this great lesson from Jesus' letters to the churches.

3. The third lesson from the letters to seven churches: *Christ wants Christians to live in purity*. Flowing from the previous point that He wants churches to watch carefully what is taught, Christ also makes it very clear that Christians are not to live by the worldly standards around them. This is precisely the difficulty in Pergamum and Thyatira where they were allowing teachers to approve of eating meat offered to idols and committing fornication. Such teaching will lead to immorality among Christians. Like these churches, we are under the same pressure. None of us likes to be different from the people around us. For early

Christians, the temptation was to take part in the social custom of attending a feast at the temple of the local pagan god. This is where the people were. To avoid this exciting entertainment of eating a banquet with meat offered to idols and participating in sexual engagements with the temple priestesses meant becoming an outcast. So some Christians found a way to justify such activities even though they were clearly forbidden by the apostles and prophets. These false teachers said, "You can do these things just with your body and, since the body is nothing and is destined to decay, that will not be sinful or harmful." So they rationalized and participated. They said they could be Christians without having to separate themselves from the practices of the world around them.

Often we seek the same solution. "Everybody else is doing it." "Let's don't be extremists, or radicals, or old-fogies." "How can we reach out to people if we isolate ourselves from them?" Our tendency to let the world set our moral standards will, like those in Pergamum and Thyatira, lead us not only into immorality, but ultimately into abandoning the faith. So the words of Christ still ring today as He says He will punish both those who lead others and those who participate in the immorality of the world around us.

4. The fourth lesson from the letters to the churches: *Christ wants Christians to grow in service.* Christ is not only interested in what we believe and how we live, but also in how we serve. Just as He showed the heart of a servant and said He came not to be served but to serve, even so He calls us to be servants. He commended the church in Thyatira because "you are now doing more than you did at first" (2:19). Here was a church that was growing in service. Christ wants to say that to us all: you are doing more now to serve me than you were doing last year or the year before. Of course, our situations change; we grow older, we have more or less money, we have changing responsibilities. But according to our opportunities, Christ wants us to be growing in our service to Him— teaching more, visiting more, writing more cards and notes of appreciation, sharing more of what we have with others, caring more for others,

grading more correspondence courses, doing more for our families. Maybe for you, more means doing it better or with a better attitude.

To the church in Philadelphia, Christ said, "I have set before you an open door which none can shut" (3:8). And He has set before all of us such open doors of opportunity. There is no church and no individual Christian that does not have opportunities. One young lady decided to have church members sign get well cards and she took them to each patient in her small town hospital. One elderly man was so touched that he and his wife came to church and were soon baptized along with others in their family. A man who ate lunch in the same café each day visited with the waitresses and occasionally mentioned where he went to church and invited them to go. Although none had come, when one of them learned she had cancer, she wanted to talk with someone who was religious. She spoke to the man who had told her where he went to church. Eventually the man's preacher taught the woman and three of her friends in a Bible study and all four were baptized. Christ does, indeed, set before us doors of opportunity and we must look to find them and meet the challenge.

Unfortunately, Christ did not find all of the churches doing so well in service. To the church in Ephesus, Christ wrote that they had left their first love and needed to repent and do their first works. Otherwise He would remove their lampstand. How did He know they had left their first love? They no longer did their first works. Obviously Christ sees what we do as a way to demonstrate our love. And isn't it always that way? The young man who has fallen in love looks carefully to see what he can do for his girlfriend. The wife who loves her husband delights in doing what makes him happy. And Christ expects His churches to be showing their love by their works.

Christ condemned the church in Laodicea by calling them "lukewarm" (3:16). Cold water has a value and so does hot water, but lukewarm water is useless. Since they were not being of service to Him, they were as useless as lukewarm water. Let us never fail to serve so that such a description would fit us.

Finally, to the church in Sardis, Jesus wrote, "you have a reputation of being alive, but you are dead. Wake up! Strengthen what remains and is about to die, for I have not found your deeds complete in the sight of my God" (3:1-2). A reputation for starting things but not finishing them. Some thought they were serving, but truly they were not. Christ might have been "reading in their church bulletin" of the many things they had planned and wanted to do—so they had a good reputation—but the truth was that they never brought their good intentions to fruition. So, He says, you are dead.

Note the range. To Sardis, you are dead; to Laodicea, you are lukewarm; to Ephesus, you have left your first love. But to Philadelphia, you have opportunities before you and to Thyatira, your last works are more than your first. Let us serve so Christ can say of us, we are using our opportunities and are growing in our service to Him.

5. The fifth lesson from the letters: *Christ wants Christians to be ready for persecution.* In five of the seven letters, Christ mentions persecution in one way or another. Ephesus had endured hardships for His name. Smyrna had experienced afflictions and slander, and prison and persecution are coming. Pergamum already had a martyr, Antipas, and others had also refused to renounce His name. Thyatira has persevered. To Philadelphia He writes that an "hour of trial" is about to come to test those who live on the earth." And he commends them because they have not denied His name and assures them their persecutors will someday bow before them.

Christians in Asia Minor had been under persecution and more was on the way. Christ is writing to help them be ready for the difficult times that are coming. How would you react to word from Jesus that you were about to undergo suffering for Him? Would you leave? Would you hide? Would you renounce? Obviously Christ is writing to encourage faithfulness even in the midst of trial.

I once read a letter from a preacher in Saigon, Vietnam, who was telling of the ways Christians there were preparing for the time when the Communists would take over their city. They were finding ways to communicate secretly and were developing ways to meet with other Christians when the order came they could not assemble as a church. They were even memorizing much Scripture against the time when their Bibles might be taken away.

Christ writes these churches to prepare them for the worst. In the letter to Smyrna He says, "Be faithful even to the point of death and I will give you the crown of life" (2:10). He means they are to be faithful even if it means dying, not just to be faithful until you die.

So, Christ is preparing the seven churches for the persecution to come and would have us to be prepared, as well, for persecution we may some day experience. Our persecution will not likely be life-threatening, although there are Christians even now facing such a danger. Our persecution is more likely to come in the form of ridicule, losing a job, being left out of things, sacrificing friendships, and even abuse. Whatever our persecution, we should be as ready for it as the early Christians were to face their opposition. "All who live godly in Christ Jesus shall suffer persecution" (2 Timothy 3:12). Our commitment must be strong enough to live for Him or to die for Him.

6. The sixth lesson from the letters to the churches: *Christ wants Christians to know they can be lost.* Sometimes the question is raised as to whether once a person is saved can that person ever be lost. After all, Paul says in Romans 8:39 that nothing can separate us from the love of Christ. And John writes that "He who has the Son has life" (1 John 5:12). John even says we "may know" that we have eternal life (1 John 5:13). So can one who has become a child of God through the new birth available in Christ someday sin so as to be lost?

Chapters two and three of Revelation answer that question very clearly. One who has been saved can be lost. To those in Ephesus He threatened, "If you do not repent, I will come to you and remove your lampstand from its place" (2:5). To those in Smyrna, He made receiving the crown conditioned upon being faithful: "Be faithful, even to the point of death, and I will give you the crown of life" (2:10). He charged those in Pergamum to repent or else He would "fight them with the sword of my mouth" (2:16). To those in Thyatira who followed the woman Jezebel into immorality, He warns that he will strike them dead and those who do not have this teaching must "hold on" to what they have (2:22-25). To Sardis, Christ again calls for repentance and obedience and says if they do not He will come upon them like a thief (3:3). Those who have not soiled their clothes, however, will walk with Him in white. Of these faithful ones He says, "I will never blot out his name from the book of life, but will acknowledge his name before my Father and his angels" (2:10). Surely if those written into Christ's book of the saved could not be blotted out, Christ would have made no such statement. And to the church in Philadelphia he urges, "Hold on to what you have, so that no one will take your crown" (3:11).

If those in the church, those saved by Christ's blood, cannot be lost, then why would he urge them to repent, to hold fast, to obey, to be faithful. While Satan cannot take those who are Christ's from Him, those who are Christ's can take themselves away by unfaithfulness. As Peter put it, those who "have escaped the corruption of the world by knowing our Lord and Savior Jesus Christ and are again entangled in it and overcome, they are worse off at the end then they were at the beginning" (2 Peter 2:20). Thus, Peter says it is better not to have become a Christian than after having done so, to return to the world. John put it this way: "But if we walk in the light, as he is in the light, we have fellowship with one another, and he blood of Jesus his Son, purifies us from all sin" (1 John 1:7). In the previous verse, John says that Christians who do not live by the truth, "walk in darkness." So Christians walk in the light when they live by the truth. When they sin, as all of us will sometimes do, they repent and confess the sin and continue to walk in the light as Christ forgives them. But if they quit trying to live by the truth and do not repent of their sins, then they leave the light for the darkness. Christ wants the seven churches to know they must keep on living for Him and not fall back into sin.

But Christ does not leave His churches on a note of warning; rather He closes each letter with a wonderful promise. And so to the last teaching from the letters.

7. The seventh lesson from the letters: *Christ will richly reward those who overcome.* Every letter, even those containing severe warnings, closes with the promise of a reward. You may look through catalogs with wonderful products you would like to have, but no catalog offers what Christ promises to those of His who overcome. To Ephesus: you can eat of the

tree of life in the paradise of God. You can live forever. To Smyrna: you will receive the crown of life and you will not be hurt in the second death. The crown of life signifies eternal victory with Christ and escaping the second death means to avoid eternal punishment in the Lake of Fire. To Pergamum: I will give you the hidden manna and a stone with your name written on it. You will have the spiritual manna to sustain you as the Israelites had the physical manna to survive in the wilderness and you will be special like those whose stones are chosen. To Thyatira: you will receive the iron scepter to join me in my conquest over the nations and I will give you the morning star. To those being oppressed by the nations, having the promise of someday being victorious over them would have held special meaning and to receive the morning star means to possess Christ Himself. To Sardis: you will be dressed in white and I will acknowledge you before the Father. You shall wear the white robe indicating your purity and, thus, I can confess you before God. To Philadelphia: I will make you a pillar in God's temple and will write on you the name of God, and God's city, and my own new name. You will be a permanent, unmovable part of God's special place with the honor of recognition from the Father and the Son. To Laodicea: you can sit down with me on my throne, thus joining in my victory.

What a glorious list of promises—all focusing on eternal life with God and Christ in heaven. Wearing white, standing as a pillar in God's temple, sitting with Christ in victory, eating of the tree of life. Christ wants Christians to be people of hope. Yes, unfaithfulness can take these things away, but those who overcome have great rewards in store.

Note that in every case, the reward is only promised to those who "overcome." This word does not suggest perfection, but it does suggests strong effort. We must be trying. We must be walking in the light as He is in the light so His blood can be cleansing us from our sins (1 John 1:7). But if we leave the light for the road of darkness, we should expect no such rewards. The Greek word translated overcome is a word known to everyone. It is the word *nike*, victory. Those who overcome are "*nikes*," they are winners. Like the Olympic athletes, they have run with patience the race set before them and have now been rewarded with the favor of God. Christ wants His people to live in this hope, the hope of great victory. Regardless of how dark our circumstances in this life may be, we are sustained by the hope of being with Christ in heaven. Keep focused on the hope which lies at the end of the race.

So we find these seven great themes running though Christ's letters to the churches. Such important messages for them in their time and circumstances! And great lessons for us today! While we do not face exactly the threat they did, we have our times of trial as well. Christ calls on us to be faithful to His Word, to live in purity, to grow in service, to be ready for persecution, to know we can be lost, and to expect great rewards. He wants us to understand that He knows and loves each of us and wants to walk with us each step of the way so He can lead us to the home He is preparing for us. Just think! Someday we can sit with those redeemed from these seven churches and talk with them about their trials and the victories they won. But only if we, like them, overcome in the name of Christ.

LESSON 3
THRONES, SEALS, AND TRUMPETS

REVELATION 4-11

Chapters 1 through 3 of Revelation provide the introduction or prologue to the book. There we learned the apostle John, while exiled on the Island of Patmos, received a message from Christ which he was to record and send to seven churches in Asia Minor. It was a message of great importance for them because it was about a major persecution the Roman Empire was soon to initiate. Christ wanted them to be prepared for such a threat to wipe out the church. In the letters to each church, He discusses their strengths and weaknesses and encourages them to hold fast during the difficult days soon to come.

CHAPTER 4: THE STAGE SETTING

As we come to chapter 4, we reach the beginning of the storyline of the book. Revelation is actually a drama, a play in two acts. This sermon will cover Act 1 of the drama and the next three lessons will cover Act II. So imagine you have gone to the theatre and are anticipating the opening of the play. As we start chapter 4, the curtain rises and John describes the stage on which the action will take place. As we look through "a door into heaven," we see in the very center is a throne and the one seated on it is like a beautiful jewel, and around the throne is an emerald looking rainbow. All commentators agree that this glorious throne is the throne of God where He sits and reigns. Next we see twenty-four more thrones circling the one where God sits. These thrones are for "elders." These are never specifically identified although some conjecture they are the 12 patriarchs and the 12 apostles. In any case, they add to the grandeur of the throne room of God which features not one throne but twenty-five.

Near God's throne are four living creatures, cherubim, high ranking angels. These four creatures cry out day and night, "Holy, holy, holy, is the Lord God, the Almighty, who was and who is and who is to come" (4:8). The twenty-four elders join in the praise, casting their crowns before Him and saying, "Worthy are you, our Lord and our God, to receive the glory and honor and power" (4:11).

But this is only the start of what we see taking place on the stage. Chapter 4 also says there are seven lamps of fire burning before God's throne. These represent the seven Spirits of God, or the Holy Spirit. There is also a body of water, like a crystal sea. And in Revelation 6:9, we learn there is an altar for sacrifice and in 8:3 there is an altar of incense, and in 11:19, the ark of the covenant is mentioned. So a lampstand with seven lamps, an altar of incense, an ark of the covenant, a body of water, and an altar for sacrifice. Anything come to mind? Sounds much like the tabernacle or temple, doesn't it? And that should come as no surprise for Hebrews 8:2-5 and 9:23-26 suggest that what was in the tabernacle was a copy of what was in heaven. Just why each of these objects is part of the heavenly furnishing we don't know but they do represent concepts related to our salvation and we shall see what part they play in the Revelation story.

But there is still more to what we see on the stage as we anticipate the start of the main action. In Revelation 5:11, we learn that around all of what we have seen so far are gathered ten thousand times ten thousand angels, and thousands and thousands of them. So the heavenly host of angles is part of this scene, adding their praise to God. And, in addition, 5:13 says that all created beings in heaven, and on the earth, and under the earth are also present for this story and they, also, are crying out in praise.

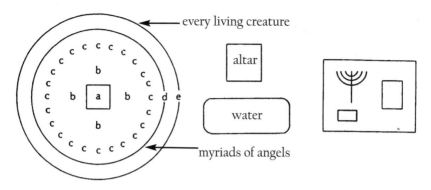

So as we look about the stage, we see the great throne room of God where He (a) is surrounded by twenty-four more thrones (c), by cherubim shouting His praises (b), and by all angels (d) and all created beings (e) who join the chorus to honor Him. Think of the power of this image to persecuted Christians in the early days of the church—with no political power, open and vulnerable, outcasts and persecuted. The God they serve sits in a greater throne room than the Roman emperors do and He has far more power than those earthly rulers who are persecuting them.

CHAPTER 5: THE SCROLL AND THE LAMB

As we arrive at chapter 5, with the picture of the stage in mind, the storyline of Revelation begins. The one seated on the throne has in His hand a scroll, sealed with seven seals. The large number of seals suggests the importance of the message and also means that only one with great authority can break the seals and open the scroll. The cry goes out for someone to come and open the scroll, but no one is found worthy. John begins to cry because he is so anxious for someone to open it. One of the elders, however, comforts John and tells him: Don't cry for someone is coming who can open the scroll. He is the lion of the tribe of Judah, the root of David. And about that time, John sees a lamb standing before the throne. The lamb has seven eyes, which are the seven Spirits of God, thus representing that the Lamb has the fullness of the Spirit. The Lamb also has seven horns, representing great power. This lamb looks as if he has been killed and is now alive again.

So do we have enough clues to identify the lamb? He is the lion of Judah and of the root of David. He pictured as a very powerful lamb, full of the Holy Spirit, who has been killed, sacrificed, and is now alive again—standing before the throne of God. Surely no one would miss this one. Says lamb, means Jesus!

And note what we learn from this description. Where are we in the lifespan of the Son of God? Has He been to earth yet? Yes. Has He been killed yet? Yes. Has He been raised from the dead yet? Yes. Is He in heaven again? Yes. The story of Revelation begins, then, at a point in time after the death, burial, resurrection, and ascension of Christ.

As the Lamb is recognized as the one who soon will open the seals on the scroll, song breaks out. The elders, the angels, and all living creatures praise Him and sing about His worthiness to open the scrolls. They declare that He was killed and that with His death, He purchased unto God with His blood people from every tribe, tongue, people, and nation and made them to be a priestly kingdom unto God. Christ's kingdom, then, exists and people are already in it. His kingdom is operational when Revelation was written, and those who hold citizenship in this kingdom are priests. On this note of high praise for the Lamb, chapter 5 closes.

CHAPTER 6: OPENING THE SEALS

As chapter 6 begins, the Lamb, Christ, takes the scroll from the hand of God and begins to open the seals. This scroll contains the story about to be revealed though the chapters 6 through 11 of Revelation. As each seal is opened, another part of the story is exposed. As we understand the message of these chapters, then, we will know what is in the scroll. Opening the seals in sequence is just a dramatic way of introducing the content of this part of the book. Since the seventh seal will introduce seven trumpets, the story revealed by the seven seals is finished when the seventh trumpet is sounded near the end of chapter 11.

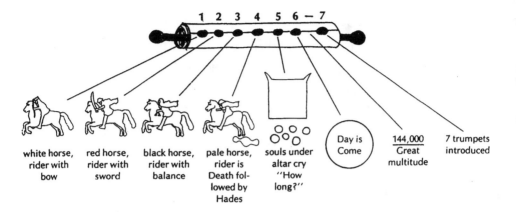

| 1 | 2 | 3 | 4 | 5 | 6 — 7 |

| white horse, rider with bow | red horse, rider with sword | black horse, rider with balance | pale horse, rider is Death followed by Hades | souls under altar cry "How long?" | Day is Come | 144,000 Great multitude | 7 trumpets introduced |

As Christ opens the first seal, one of the four living creatures calls "Come," and a rider on a white horse comes on the stage. This rider has a bow and is given a crown and is told to go forth and conquer.

Christ opens the second seal and a second living creature calls another rider to come. He is on a red horse and the rider is given a large sword signifying power to take peace from the earth.

When Christ opens the third seal, the third living creature calls a rider on a black horse who has a pair of scales in his hand. He is told to measure wheat and barley at high prices. Thus this third rider brings scarcity of food, and thus, economic distress.

When Christ opens the fourth seal, the fourth living creature says "Come," and a pale horse whose rider is Death comes across the stage, with Hades following close behind to pick up after Death. They are given power over a fourth of the earth to kill by sword, famine, plagues, and wild beasts.

Having seen these four horsemen ride across the stage, we must pause and ask what they mean. Remember, it says four horsemen, but what does it mean? Well, what do we know? We know they ride where God sits on the throne. We know they are called into action by one of God's highest ranking angels. We know that since an angel calls each one, it is by the authority of God they are given their power to affect the earth with conquest, war, economic troubles, and difficulties of other kinds. These horsemen, then, are not tools of Satan; they are, rather, agents of God. They signify God's power to affect the affairs of nations. In the Old Testament, God had said He would use Assyrian power to afflict the kingdom of Israel for their idolatry. God had said He would use Babylon to afflict Judah for their disobedience. God has always taken a hand in the rise and fall of nations. After all, Paul said to the Athenians that the God he is telling about is the one who determines the times set for nations and the exact place where they should live (Acts 17:26). Who brought down the iron curtain? Give Ronald Reagan some credit but God's power was the real force behind the fall of communism. His time for them ran out.

So, at the very beginning of the story, Christ reveals to the readers of the book that God is in control. He sits on a beautiful throne in the midst of awesome power. He gives the riders their power to use conquest, war, economic distress, and other forces to make nations rise and fall. Not only has He done it before, but He can do it again. The Christians in the seven churches can have faith in the power of God over nations, even though they are going through a time of persecution. So in the four horsemen, God parades His power.

Next, the Lamb opens the fifth seal and we see under the altar of sacrifice the souls of those who have been killed because of "the word of God and the testimony they had maintained" (6:9). Later, this testimony is called the testimony of Jesus (12:17). These, then, are early martyrs, killed because they will not relent in their testimony of faith in Jesus. And now in the spirit realm with God, they are asking a question. "How long, Sovereign Lord, holy and true, until you judge the inhabitants of the earth and avenge our blood?" (6:10). They know that the force who killed them continues and they have just seen God's parade of power over nations. So they ask God to "judge" and "avenge" their blood. *Remember those two words: judge and avenge.* They are not asking for revenge but are seeking justice. It is not right that one who has killed God's people should go unpunished and, for the time, that seems to be happening. So, knowing God has the power to do so, they ask Him, "how long" until you act to rectify this wrong?

From this event we learn more about the timetable in Revelation. In chapter 5, we saw that Christ had died, had been raised, and was back in heaven. This verse extends our understanding of the time. Now the church has been established and a significant number have already been killed. These early martyrs cry out for God to bring their persecutor to justice. So the story of Revelation is occurring in the early days of the church.

In the next verses, 6:10 and 11, we find God's answer to the martyrs' question. He gives each of them a white robe and tells them to wait a little longer until more of their fellow servants and brothers have also been martyred. So, there has been persecution and there will be more. *These verses are the most important ones in the book for providing the basic theme of Revelation.* The book is actually written to answer this question the martyrs ask, "How long before God ends the persecution and brings the persecutor down to defeat?" The answer is that the persecution will continue for a while but then God will end it and destroy the persecuting nation. We will be coming back to these verses later as we see the story of the book unfold.

Remember the martyr's question: How long before you *judge* the persecutor and *avenge* our blood he has shed?

Now Christ opens the sixth seal and, according to 6:12-14, there is an earthquake, the sun goes dark, the moon looks red, and stars fall. The sky rolls up like a scroll and leaders of the earth look for caves and rocks to hide in. They are so afraid that they call on the mountains and rocks to fall on them to hide them from the face of God and the Lamb. The great day of their wrath has come and who can stand? We must remind ourselves that we are in the midst of a figurative book. These things are what it says. But what does it mean?

We get a very important clue to the meaning of these striking events when we recognize that each of the expressions in this passage is directly from the Old Testament. Isaiah 2:12-22 likens the coming destruction of Judah and Jerusalem to the time of a great earthquake when men hide in caves. Isaiah 13:9-16 compares the fall of Babylon to a time when the sun is darkened, the moon and stars cease to shine. Isaiah

34:4 says the fall of Edom will be like the heavens being rolled together as a scroll. Hosea 10:8 describes the fall of Samaria as a time when the people cry to the mountains to fall on them. And Joel 2:28-32 speaks of the sun being darkened and the moon turning to blood in a prophesy about the coming of the new age and the end of the Jewish nation.

So each element of what happens at the sixth seal is a *direct quotation* of a figurative statement from the Old Testament and each of these scriptures was speaking of *the fall of a nation*: Judah, Babylon, Edom, Samaria, and the Jewish nation of Jesus' day. So what do we learn here? Revelation 6:17 and 7:1 indicate that the day of God's wrath has arrived, but it has not yet been unleashed. When it is, it will be like the time when God brought down nations in the past. This story, now getting started, then, will describe the way God will bring down a nation, even as He brought down nations before. The martyrs have asked, "How long" before you judge and avenge and God says He will meet their request to defeat their persecutor, even though it will take a while to come to pass.

These Old Testament expressions, then, are like a drum roll of God's wrath as He poured it out on nations in the past. The message is that God is about to do it again, and when He gets ready to make His move, who can stand? And, of course, no one can.

CHAPTER 7: THE INTERLUDE

We now come to an *interlude* between the opening of the sixth and seventh seals and during this break, God wants to do something very important. According to verses 1 through 3, God wishes to hold the action until he has accomplished something important He wishes to do. "Don't start yet," He says. But what does He want to do?

Verse 3 says, "Do not harm the land or the sea or the trees until we put a seal on the forehands of the servants of our God." God holds back the action, then, until He puts His mark on His people. The identifying mark will be His name written on their foreheads (14:1). So God is going to write His name on those who are His.

Actually, in the story of Revelation there are those on the good side and those on the bad side. Ever watch a Western? The good side guys will wear the "white hats" of God's name on their forehead. The bad guys, we learn in chapter 13, will wear the "black hats" of the mark of the beast.

So how many of His people will God seal? The text says He will mark twelve thousand out of each of the twelve tribes of Israel, and thus a total of 144,000. That is what it says. What does it mean? We know that in the book of Revelation we deal with not only symbolic animals, but with symbolic numbers as well. We know, too, that those marked are "the servants of our God." So who are the servants of God at the time of the writing of this book? When Paul writes the Romans, about thirty years before Revelation was written, he speaks of the true offspring of Abraham as not the natural children but, rather, the children of promise, that is, Christians. In Galatians 6:16, Paul speaks of Christians as "the Israel of God." In Philippians 3:3, similarly, Paul speaks of those who follow Jesus as "the circumcision." So by the time John is writing Revelation, the true Israel is not fleshly Israel but spiritual Israel, the church. When Revelation here speaks of 144,000 Jews as the people of God, then, it is using Israel in a figurative sense to mean God's people at the time he writes; that is, the church.

But what is the meaning of the number 144,000? In modern times we use some numbers in a figurative sense. So many consider thirteen as an unlucky number, for example, that most hotels do not number a floor as thirteen. Look at the elevator numbers. They will skip that number. Eleven, twelve, fourteen, fifteen. So the floor numbered fourteen is actually the thirteenth floor. If you want to avoid floor thirteen, don't stay on the one numbered fourteen! We think of seven as a lucky number. In the ancient world, even much more was made of the symbolism of numbers. The number twelve was a number for completeness and so to think of that number multiplied by itself would make 144, which meant *very* complete. The number 1,000 was also thought by them, as by us, as a number suggesting fullness or totality. "I've told you a thousand times not to tell me that." So for God to say He would put His mark on twelve times twelve times a thousand of His people, 144,000 of them, He was saying that He would number very completely, He would not miss any. He will mark each and every one of those who is His. He will put His seal on every member of the church who is about to undergo persecution.

In this symbolism, God is conveying to the seven churches of Asia that He will put His protecting arm around all of them. They are His as much as if they had been branded with His name on their foreheads. Even if they are martyred in the persecution, they are still His. What a comfort to those about to enter a time of a vicious attack on the church! They belong to God as much as if He had marked them with His name. And note that these Christians are on earth for in verse 3 He says, "Do not harm the land or the sea or the trees until we put a seal on the foreheads of the servants of our God." Later we will see the 144,000 in heaven, after their martyrdom, but now, before the time of intense persecution, they are on earth.

So during the interlude between the sixth and seventh seals, God holds back the action until He can mark those who are His, the church, on earth, about to undergo a terrible time of persecution.

Also during the time between the sixth and seventh seals, we are given a look into heaven (7:9-17). There we see a great multitude who have come out of the great tribulation. They are wearing white robes and so are those souls we saw under the altar in Revelation 6:9. In this scene, these martyrs, who have washed their robes in the blood of the Lamb, are serving before the throne of God. Never again will they hunger or thirst or feel the heat of the sun, and God shall wipe away all their tears. Those on earth, about to undergo persecution, are here given a view of those who have experienced martyrdom already. They see that the early martyrs now serve before the throne of God where He gives them freedom from all pain and sorrow. What an encouragement this must have been to those soon to suffer persecution for their Lord!

This visual gives us a chance to review the events of the opening of the seals—the four horsemen which display God's power among the nations, the souls under the altar crying out "How long?," the earthquake and astronomical events of the sixth seal indicating God will again act in the affairs of a nation, and the interlude when the 144,000 people of God are sealed and the early martyrs serve him.

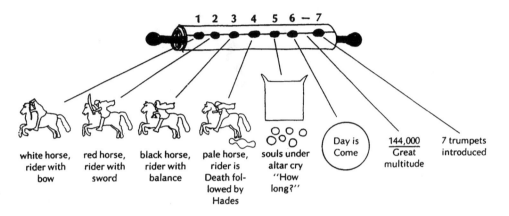

white horse, rider with bow	red horse, rider with sword	black horse, rider with balance	pale horse, rider is Death followed by Hades	souls under altar cry "How long?"	Day is Come	144,000 Great multitude	7 trumpets introduced

CHAPTER 8: THE FIRST FOUR TRUMPETS

Now the Lamb opens the seventh and last seal holding the scroll which He took from the hand of God. To emphasize the solemn moment, there is half-an-hour of silence in heaven. Then come seven angels, and each is given a trumpet. In preparation for the sounding of these trumpets, an angel comes with a golden censer to the altar of incense. As he places the incense on the altar, he mixes it with the ascending prayers of the saints. A beautiful picture of the sweet smell of the prayers of Christians going before God!

The angels with the trumpets now begin to blow. Just as when each seal was opened an event took place, with each trumpet blast some event occurs. What shall we make of the symbolism of sounding trumpets? Obviously these trumpets are not being blown for entertainment or making music. In ancient times, the blowing of a trumpet was often for warning. Men stood on the top of the wall of a city prepared to blow a trumpet to spread the word of a coming enemy. In 1 Corinthians 14:8, Paul speaks of a trumpet being blown to warn people to prepare for war. Such was the common meaning of the sounding of a trumpet.

Another indication that the trumpets are blown as a warning is that as each is sounded, only one-third of the area named is affected by the plague named. Since only *partial* rather than *complete* destruction comes from the sounding trumpets, they are intended to signal a warning.

Still a third indication that the trumpets are used here to warn comes from the results of the warning stated after the sounding of the sixth trumpet. In Revelation 9:20-21, we learn of the response to the trumpets. The one against whom they are sounded "does not repent." Rather he continues with his worship of demons and murders, and sorcery, sexual immorality, and theft.

Since the angels blowing the trumpets are God's servants, they sound God's warning. They warn someone engaged in false religion and immorality and who, after the warnings, does not change. Who could this be? From our earlier study, we know that this book is about the persecution of Christians by the Roman Empire. We also know that God told the martyrs that more would undergo persecution before He brought that to an end (6:10). So the warning from the trumpets is to the Roman Empire and by telling what happens as each trumpet sounds, God suggests how He will provide the warning.

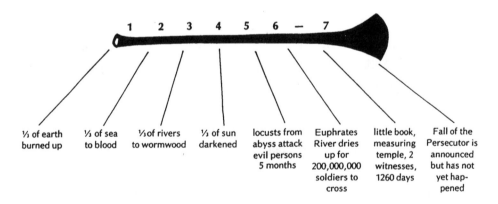

1	2	3	4	5	6	—	7
⅓ of earth burned up	⅓ of sea to blood	⅓ of rivers to wormwood	⅓ of sun darkened	locusts from abyss attack evil persons 5 months	Euphrates River dries up for 200,000,000 soldiers to cross	little book, measuring temple, 2 witnesses, 1260 days	Fall of the Persecutor is announced but has not yet happened

With the sounding of the first trumpet, hail and fire mixed with blood are hurled down on the earth and this causes a third of the earth to be burned up with its trees and grass. So, one-third of the *land* portion of the world is burned. The second trumpet causes a huge mountain to burn and, when it is thrown into the sea, one-third of the *sea* turns to blood and a third of the creatures of the sea die and one-third of the ships are destroyed. One-third of the sea turns to blood. The third trumpet is blown and a star named Wormwood falls into the *rivers* and a third of these become bitter and many die from drinking this water. One-third of the rivers become bitter. The fourth angel blows his trumpet and a third of the sun, a third of the moon and a third of the stars are darkened. One-third of the sun, moon, and stars are darkened, thus affecting the *sky*.

So, let's see what we know about the first four trumpets. They represent warnings against the persecutor and they affect one-third of the land, the seas, the rivers, and the sky. We know we are dealing with symbols here because one burning mountain could not possibly cause one-third of all the earth's seas to become blood and one actual star falling could not possibly turn one-third of the earth's rivers to bitterness. So it says one-third of nature is affected. But what does it mean?

Since we know these trumpet symbols represent some type of warning to the persecutor and since land, sea, rivers, and sky represent all the aspects of nature, it seems reasonable to conclude that God is saying He will use various types of natural disasters as a means of warning. We know that natural disasters can be very sobering—a flood, a tornado, a fire, an earthquake. And God here is saying that one of His means for warning the Roman Empire to change its attitude toward the church will be to send natural disasters upon them.

What is the most famous volcanic eruption in history? Vesuvius, when it erupted on Pompeii, the resort city for Romans. When did this occur? In 79 AD. Just about the time of the writing of the book of Revelation. So, the first four trumpets of warning suggest that God will use disasters from various aspects of nature to warn the persecutor. Surely we would be mistaken to make these descriptions actual hail mixed with blood, a literal mountain, or literal blood. Rather, we see symbolism here and know that what it says should lead us to ask what it means. What it means is that God will use natural disasters of various kinds—volcanic eruptions, fires, floods, winds, earthquakes—to warn Rome to change its policy of persecution.

CHAPTER 9: THE FIFTH AND SIXTH TRUMPETS

The fifth angel blows his trumpet and a star falls to the earth. This star is given a key with which to open the Abyss. Throughout Revelation, the Abyss is the home base of evil. From the Abyss comes the beast (11:7), the Abyss will be a place of prison for the dragon (20:3) and the angel of the Abyss is named "Destroyer." In this passage (9:1-11), then, the Abyss is the place from which evil forces come. When the star opens the Abyss, there first comes out smoke and then, out of the smoke, come locusts who descend to the earth. They have heads like humans, hair like women, teeth like lions, and breastplates like iron. Their tails can sting like scorpions and with these tails they torment for five months those who do *not* have the seal of God on their foreheads. That's what it says. What does it mean? Look at the clues. The first is that these locusts come from the headquarters of evil in the book and have as their king one named Destroyer. Some think this refers to Satan. In any case, these creatures are from the evil side. Maybe I should say, "the dark side." The second clue is that the object of their torment is not the good people, those sealed by God in chapter 7, but those who do not have such a seal—that is, evil people. So the torment comes from the source of evil and afflicts those who are evil. The third clue is that the torment is only for five months. This parallels the idea of "one-third" in the earlier warnings. The period of five months would suggest a fairly limited time of torment and thus fits the idea of a warning rather than total destruction. And the locusts do not kill; they only bring pain. What shall we make of these creatures? Remember, the context is within the framework of the trumpets of warning and they come from an evil place to afflict only those who are evil.

The meaning that best fits what we know is this. Locusts coming from evil to hurt evil people suggests the idea of "evil against itself" or evil people suffering the consequences of their own evil deeds.

Sometimes those who do evil seem to prosper and not suffer bad consequences. The souls of those persecuted (6:9) thought the persecutor was not being judged and their blood was not being avenged. For this they cried out. Here the message seems to be that the time has come for the *beginning* of consequences of evil upon those who do evil. At this time, Rome was growing in its own immorality. Its emperors were men of deceit, sexual indulgence, and drunkenness. They led the nation in a growing love of violent entertainment. And the Romans were increasing their amount of emperor worship and hating Christians who refused to take part. So, God says, as part of the warning process, Rome will begin to suffer the effects of its own immorality. Long ago, Solomon had said, "Righteousness exalts a nation, but sin is a reproach to any people" (Proverbs 14:34). And now, as a warning, the Empire will begin to experience the consequences of its own evil deeds. It will experience the weakening effect of its own immorality. Evil against itself.

Now the sixth angel sounds his trumpet and we are transported to the Euphrates River. The Euphrates was famous for being the eastern-most boundary of the Roman Empire. I remember being in Germany a few years ago where I visited the museum in a fortress which marked the northern-most outpost of the Romans. On the wall was a large map of the entire Roman Empire at its largest extent. And clearly marked as its eastern boundary was the Euphrates River. As the sixth angel blows, we not only see the river but those waiting on the other side: two hundred million soldiers riding horses with heads like lions and with tails like snakes. From the horses' mouths came forth fire, and smoke, and sulfur. These are freed to come across the river and attack those inside the boundaries of the Empire. It is hard to imagine this picture: two hundred million men riding on horses with heads like lions belching out fire and smoke and sulfur. Some see this as a picture of modern warfare with the horses actually being a mechanized vehicle and they assume that the soldiers are from China since this is the only place, they say, which could produce an army of this size. We must remember, however, that we are in a symbolic book and of John's description we must ask not only what it says but what it means. *Says* two hundred million soldiers riding on unusual horses and crossing the Euphrates. *Means*, however, that God will use those forces from beyond Rome's borders to join in this time of warning. Since the Euphrates was a well-known boundary of Rome, it is clearly used here as symbolic of all its boundaries. The huge hoard of soldiers coming across would represent those tribes, such as the Goths, Visigoths, Huns, and Vandals who actually did cross Rome's boundaries to make major incursions into Roman territory. These attacks from outside forces would provide a major warning to Rome that it was vulnerable and needed to make major changes within. So the picture of the huge army crossing the Euphrates was to give a message to those who first received the book and the message was that God was going to institute a time of warning against the persecutor of the church and part of that warning would come through attacks from beyond its borders.

Now we are back to Revelation 9:20-21 to which we referred earlier. God has now said He would use three major forces to send a message of warning to the persecutor, the Roman Empire. These messages would come through natural disasters, through the effect of its own immorality on itself, and from the beginning of attacks from those beyond its borders. Now, what will be the result of such warnings? The answer is that there is no repentance. They do not stop their pagan worship or their murders or their immorality or their stealing. These practices, many of which were involved in the persecution of Christians, would go on unchecked. God gave them a chance to change and they refused. In fact, as we shall see in chapters 11, 12, and 13, they will institute a time of persecution called figuratively the 1260 days or 42 months or 3 1/2 years during which "the beast" will lead in a fierce attack on Christians.

So the martyrs have called out to God, asking "How long" before you judge our persecutor and avenge our blood. He replies, it will be a while. Then He institutes a period of warning through natural disasters, the effects of internal decay, and attacks from those outside the borders. These events could have led Rome to change its policies toward Christians, but no such changes were made. Instead, Rome will begin a more intense time of persecution. Having finished the warning process, we now come to the interlude between the sixth and seventh trumpet.

CHAPTER 10: THE ANGEL AND THE SECOND SCROLL

John sees a mighty angel coming down from heaven with a little scroll in his hand. He puts one foot on the land and one on the sea. He raises his right hand to heaven and swears by the Creator, "There shall be no more delay." God has been waiting and warning, but now there will be no more delay before He sets the final actions of this story into motion. Then John is told to eat the scroll from the angel, who tells John it will be sweet as honey in his mouth but in his stomach it will be sour. (I've been to that restaurant, but I won't tell you where it was.) John says he ate the scroll as directed and it did, indeed, taste sweet in his mouth but was sour in his stomach. Such symbolism would suggest "good news" and "bad news." The scroll, then, will contain the good news is that the delay is over and God is now ready to make His move against the persecutor, but the bad news is that it will take a while for this scenario to play out. John is told, "You must prophesy again about many peoples, nations, languages and kings" (10:11). John has almost finished his prophesying out of the first scroll. With its seven seals, the first scroll has been opened and we have seen what happened with the opening of all seven seals and are now between the sixth and seventh trumpets. The contents of this first scroll, which we have called Act 1, is about done. It is time for John to receive a second scroll which will reveal "the rest of the story" and which we will call Act 2. The contents of this scroll will start in chapter 12 as soon as the seventh angel has sounded at the end of chapter 11.

CHAPTER 11: THE TEMPLE, THE WITNESSES, AND THE ANNOUNCEMENT

Still in this time between the sixth and seventh trumpets, John is now given a reed, a long stick, with which to measure. He is told to measure the temple of God and to count the worshippers, but not to include in his measuring the outer court for it is given to the Gentiles who will trample it and the holy city for 42 months. During this time, also called 1260 days, God will give power to His two witnesses who will testify during this period. They are under attack but God protects them and they can exercise various powers. "When they have finished their testimony," the beast that comes from the Abyss kills them. Their bodies will lie in the street of "the great city" for three and a half days while those from every people, tribe, language, and nation shall gloat over them, thinking they have defeated them. Then, however, God raises up these two witnesses and takes them to heaven while their enemies look on. At that moment, an earthquake collapses a tenth of the city and seven thousand are killed while the survivors are terrified and give glory to God.

That's what it says. What does it mean? Measuring the temple while the area around it is trampled would suggest that God is protecting something from destruction while it is under attack. He will allow the attack but will not allow the object He protects to be destroyed. But what is the temple which He protects? Surely it is not the actual Jewish temple in Jerusalem, for He did not keep it from being destroyed in 70 AD. By the time Revelation was written, then, this temple was already gone. What, then, would "the temple" have suggested to the early Christians who first received this book? That is not hard to imagine. They had been told by the apostles that *the church* was now God's temple. Paul calls the church a temple in 1 Corinthians 3:16 and Peter also calls the church the temple with each Christian a stone (1 Peter 2:5). That certainly would have been the thought of those receiving the book. The church, then, will be attacked for 42 months, the period of time we have previously identified as the time of the intense Roman persecution, but it will not be destroyed because God measures (protects) it from destruction.

Now what about the two witnesses? What do we know of them? They prophesy, a term used to describe messengers under inspiration from God. They are persecuted for 1260 days, the same length of time the 42-month attack on the temple, the church. God sustains the witnesses during this time for they are like lampstands which give their light with olive trees beside them so they will not run out of oil. Not until their testimony is finished, does God allow the beast to overpower them and kill them. So they finish their job, but they are killed. Their opposition is led by the beast whom we identified earlier as the Roman Empire. Their bodies lie in the street of "the great city" for three and a half days. What city would this be? It is the city where the beast rules. It is a city which may be likened to Sodom for its immorality, to Egypt for its oppression of God's people, and to Jerusalem where Jesus was killed. The city, however, is not Sodom or Egypt or Jerusalem. It has qualities of all three. Thus it is an immoral city which opposes and kills God's people and where the beast rules. Surely this is not a difficult identification. Later in Revelation 17:18, the Harlot is called "the great city" and we have previously identified her as the city of Rome. All of these indicators certainly point to Rome, the city of the beast. Since the Roman Empire is the primary persecutor in the book and since the witnesses have been killed in an attack by the beast, which represents the Roman Empire, all of this would fit very well.

So what is the underlying message about the witnesses? These two represent the Christian witness of all of those early Christians, particularly those with prophetic powers, who were under attack by the Roman Empire but who remained faithful and continued until their job was finished. Although eventually these witnesses were martyred, God was in control to the extent that He did not let them die until their work of prophecy and getting the early church established was done. These two witnesses, then, do not represent any two particular people. They represent, rather, the witness of all the early Christians who were under attack. And, while some are being killed along the way, as a whole, their witness continues throughout the period of persecution. The beast and his followers will kill enough of them that they think they have succeeded in wiping out these witnesses and their church. The victory party, however, is short-lived because it soon becomes evident that God has "raised up" His witnesses and has taken them to heaven. This signifies that although they were under severe persecution, their mission succeeded and they will be rewarded for their work. At the moment the enemies of Christ think they have won, God begins the destruction of their city and more such destruction is coming.

During the interlude between the sixth and seventh trumpets, then, John receives the scroll to eat which allows him to prophesy further after the first scroll is completely opened. Also during the interlude, the temple, meaning the church, is protected although it will be persecuted for the 42 month period. During this same time, the witnesses continue their testimony even though under attack. And, while the Roman Empire will intensify its opposition, it will not overcome the witness of early Christians in a way that will stop their work of establishing the church. While many of them will be killed in the process, they are the eventual winners.

This is a good place to review the trumpets. As shown on the picture below, the first four trumpets affected one-third of the land which burns, one-third of the sea turns to blood, one third of the rivers are bitter from the falling of the star Wormwood, and one-third of the sky is darkened. God will use the forces of nature to warn. Then come the locusts from the headquarters of evil—evil afflicting itself. Then come the 200 million horsemen from beyond the Euphrates, suggesting the warning from outside attacks. In the interlude comes the angel with another scroll and the period of 1260 days of persecution of the witnesses.

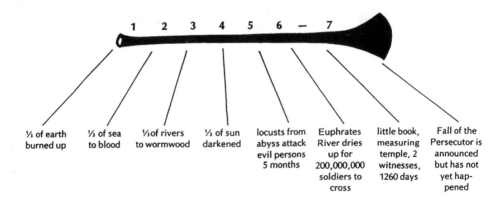

1	2	3	4	5	6	—	7

| ⅓ of earth burned up | ⅓ of sea to blood | ⅓ of rivers to wormwood | ⅓ of sun darkened | locusts from abyss attack evil persons 5 months | Euphrates River dries up for 200,000,000 soldiers to cross | little book, measuring temple, 2 witnesses, 1260 days | Fall of the Persecutor is announced but has not yet happened |

THRONES, SEALS, AND TRUMPETS

Now comes the blowing of the seventh trumpet which ends the story told in the scroll with seven seals. When the seventh angel sounds, voices in heaven shout a song of victory. God has been holding back until He decided the time was right. Now comes the announcement that God is ready to make His move. A worldly kingdom will be overtaken by the kingdom of Christ (11:15) and the twenty-four elders praise God because He is now going to use His power to reward his servants and destroy those who destroy the earth. (11:16-18). Then God's temple is opened and the ark of the covenant is visible and there is lightning, thunder, and an earthquake.

As these majestic events announce that the time has come for God to make His move against the persecutor, the curtain falls on Act 1. We have come to the end of the events under the seventh trumpet which was under the seventh seal. In chapter 4 we saw the curtain rise on the stage where the story would unfold. We saw the Lamb take the scroll and begin to open the seals. We saw the parade of God's power as the horsemen were given their orders which could affect the affairs of nations. We heard the souls of the martyrs cry their penetrating question, "How long, O Master, Holy and True, do you not judge and avenge our blood?" We heard God's answer that they must wait a while until more of their brothers had likewise suffered martyrdom. Then came the warnings to the persecutor through natural disasters, the effects of its moral corruption and from outside attacks. The warnings, however, did not bring a change and the persecutor only intensified the attack during the time symbolized by the 42 months or 1260 days. Led by the beast, later to be identified as the Roman Empire, the church is under attack and Christians testify in the midst of great opposition. While they will eventually die for the cause, their faithfulness will allow it to be well established so the beast will fail in his mission to eliminate their testimony. Finally comes the announcement that God is now ready to make His move. He will destroy the one who has been destroying. This announcement brings great excitement in heaven and, in the midst of this joy, the curtain falls on this part of the story. Although we don't yet see the conclusion of the story, we know already that the church will survive and Satan's attack will fail. It is not too early to say that Christ will win and Satan will lose. We need to be sure we are on the winning side of Christ.

LESSON 4
THE DRAGON, TWO BEASTS, AND THE HARLOT

CHAPTER 12: THE GLORIOUS WOMAN AND THE HUGE DRAGON

As we come to chapter 12, we enter a new section of Revelation. Act 1 ended on the high note of the announcement that God would now begin the process of destroying the destroyer who persecutes His people. As Act 2 begins in chapter 12, the book moves back in time a bit so there is actually an overlap with Act 1. In particular, the period of intense persecution symbolized by the 1260 days which occurred in the last part of Act 1 will now be revisited in the early part of Act 2. New characters are introduced, but the story line is the same: the persecution of God's people, how God wants them to respond and how He eventually will act.

Act 2 opens with the vision of a glorious woman, standing on the moon with the sun wrapped around her shoulders and 12 stars encircling her head. She is about to bear a child. Meanwhile, standing by to devour the child as soon as it is born, is a great, red dragon, large enough to sweep a third of the stars out of the sky with its tail. As we saw in an earlier lesson, the book clearly identifies the dragon. In Revelation 12:9 and 20:2 he is named: Satan, the devil, the one who leads the whole world astray. So, says dragon, means Satan! Everywhere you see dragon, write Satan in the margin.

The woman gives birth to a male child who is identified as the one who will rule all the nations with an iron scepter. Since this is a quotation from the second Psalm which is about the Messiah, it is clear that the child is the Christ. Satan's first attack on Christ is while He is on earth. While the details of his attack are not given here, we know Satan tried in many ways to thwart and destroy Christ while He was on earth, starting with the Bethlehem atrocity and including his manipulations to get Christ killed. All of this is compressed here in the idea that Satan wants to "devour" the child. While Satan was able to get Christ killed, he could not stop Him from doing what He came to do. To show God's protection over Christ, the text says Christ is snatched up to the throne of God. So Satan fails in his first attack of Revelation 12.

In verse 7, we begin to read about Satan's second effort to stop Christ from achieving His mission. There is now war in heaven as Michael and the good angels fight against Satan and his angels. Just how angels fight is not revealed and it is very hard to imagine. In our minds we might picture angels fighting with laser beams as in *Star Wars*, but we really have no idea how angelic beings actually carry on war. We do, however, know the outcome. Satan loses and he and his angels are thrown to the earth. Then comes a voice in heaven which says, "Now have come the salvation and the power and the kingdom of our God, and the authority of his Christ. For the accuser of our brothers, who accuses them before our God day and night, has been hurled down. They overcame him by the blood of the Lamb and by the word of their testimony" (12:10-11).

What a beautiful passage! Satan couldn't stop Christ from achieving His mission on earth so he tried to stop Him from taking His place in heaven to present His sacrifice before God. But, thanks to the work of the good angels, Satan was not successful in this attack either. With Christ now in His heavenly place, it can be said that "salvation and the power and the kingdom of our God, and the authority of our Christ" have come. Note that the kingdom has begun. Satan could not prevent Christ from taking His place of authority. And with Christ in His place at God's right hand, our accuser, Satan, is thrown down. We now can overcome Satan by the blood of the Lamb. Without the forgiveness available through Jesus, Satan could accuse me and make it stick for I would be guilty. With the sacrificial work of Jesus now done and presented before the throne, however, my sins can be forgiven. No longer can Satan accuse me for I am counted as innocent through the blood of the Lamb. Thus, Satan loses round two.

In verse 13, Satan begins his third attack. This time he goes after the woman who gave birth to the child. We shall wait a bit to identify her because more helpful details come a little later. Satan chases her to harm her but God gives her two wings like those of an eagle so she can fly to a place of safety for a time, times, and half a time. If we take "time" to mean "year," this length of time equals three and a half years, the same duration as the 42 months or 1260 days. Just as God protected the "temple" during a 42-month attack, and as He protected the witnesses through a 1260-day attack, He now protects the woman during a three-and-a-half-year attack. All three of these, of course, are the same period although spoken of in different ways. So Satan loses round three and is enraged because he cannot harm the woman.

Always persistent, Satan now prepares for round four. In Revelation 12:17, the text says He now makes war against the children or offspring of the woman—"those who obey God's commandments and hold to the testimony of Jesus." Having failed to stop Christ on earth or in heaven and having failed to harm the woman, Satan now will attack the children of the woman, Christians, those who obey Christ and hold to the testimony of Jesus. To help him in this attack on individual Christians he will bring up two allies, as chapter 13 will tell us. There the story is told of this fourth effort of Satan.

Before going on, however, we should pause to identify the woman. What clues do we have? She obviously is greater than a human being because she stands on the moon with the sun around her shoulders. In some way, she is the mother of Jesus. When attacked by Satan, God gives her wings so she may fly to safety. And Christians are said to be her children. What could match these clues? Not Mary. Although she gave birth to Jesus, she never stood on the moon or got eagles' wings to fly into the desert. Not the Jewish nation. While they could be said to have given birth to Christ, they could hardly be described as the mother of the church when, as a group, they rejected Jesus as the Messiah and engaged in their own persecution of Christians. And besides, the glorious figure of the woman and the fact that she is given wings to fly clearly indicate that the woman is not just some human being or a group of human beings. If not these, then what? What could be pictured as a glorious woman standing on the moon, who gives birth to Jesus, whom Satan wishes to harm, and who is the mother of all Christians. An answer which fits all of these is this: "the eternal plan of God." Romans 8:28 speaks of those called according to "His purpose," His plan. The plan of God, formed before the foundation of the earth and which He gradually revealed to human beings (Ephesians 1:4-10) gave birth to Christ, was something Satan wanted to thwart, and can be said to have given birth to all Christians. We are the children, the offspring, of God's plan. So Satan's third attack was to stop God's plan as a whole from going into effect, and God refuses to let this happen. But God will allow Satan to embark on the fourth attack, to severely test individual Christians by persecution. And it is this fourth attack that is now the topic of chapter 13.

CHAPTER 13: THE TWO BEASTS PERSECUTE

As we begin chapter 13, we are coming to the heart of the story of Revelation. Having failed in his first three attempts to stop Jesus from being able to provide salvation, Satan now begins this fourth effort. His plan, in a nutshell, is this. He will mount a heavy persecution of Christians, so strong, in fact, that he hopes either to kill all Christians or drive them into denial of their faith. If he can achieve this, it will not matter that he failed in his other attempts. It only takes the span of one generation to push the message about Jesus into extinction. So he will try to persecute the church out of existence. With no one left to tell the story, it will not matter that Jesus died to make forgiveness possible. But how shall he mount such a persecution? What power shall he use as his agent?

As chapter 13 begins, Satan brings up an agent up to do his bidding. This power is pictured as a beast who comes from the sea. He has ten horns and seven heads. His body is like that of a leopard, his mouth like a lion's, and his feet like those of a bear. These are clues to his identity.  But there is more. He blasphemes God; he exercises his authority for 42 months; he makes war with the saints and conquers them; he has authority over every tribe, people, language and nation; and everyone on earth worships the beast, all except those written in the Lamb's book of life (13:5-9). In chapter seventeen, we have additional clues. Here the seven heads are said to represent seven kings, five of whom are past, one of whom exists at the time of the writing, and another is yet to come. Finally, the seven heads are also said to represent seven hills on which sits the woman who rides the beast.

That's what it says. What does it mean? Here is what the clues have told us. The beast is a world-wide political power, reigning over many nations. It is led by kings or emperors and one of them is in power when John is writing Revelation. It uses its universal power to do Satan's bidding to persecute (make war on) Christians. People all over the world worship the beast as god. The woman who rides him, who is called "the great city," sits on seven hills. And the beast is like the fourth beast of Daniel 7 who represents the fourth of Daniel's kingdoms, for it also has ten horns and is seen to be made up of parts of the previous kingdoms of the Babylonians, Medes and Persians, and the Greeks. This beast with ten horns in Daniel is commonly thought to represent the Roman Empire.

As we saw in our opening lesson, only the Roman Empire can fit all these characteristics. It was in power at the time John wrote Revelation. It had power over all the earth and used its power against Christians. Roman citizens, except Christians, engaged in worship of the emperor and the city of Rome was built on seven hills. And the ten-horned beast in Daniel was the Roman Empire. The match is very strong and most commentators agree that this beast represents the Roman Empire whom Satan will use in his effort to persecute the church out of existence.

But why will the Roman Empire have such a dislike for the church? They have many religions among their people. Why will they pick on Christianity? To ensure that the beast, the Roman Empire, has reason to persecute Christians, Satan brings up a second beast (13:11-17).

This beast, with two horns like a lamb, comes up with the first beast in chapter 13 and goes down to defeat with him in chapter 19 and so the two exist together. This beast speaks like a dragon and so serves Satan. This beast works under the authority of the first beast and so does his bidding. The sole function of the second beast, we are told, is to set up statues of the heads of the first beast and to require people to worship them. Thus, the second beast sets up images of the emperors of Rome and forces people to worship them. Those who agree to worship the emperors get a mark to show they have done so. If they refuse to worship, and so do not have the identifying mark, they are unable to buy or sell and even are killed.

Such a description would have been an easy identification for Christians from the end of first century and into the second and third centuries. During this period, there was a strong effort to get people to worship the Roman emperor. Huge temples were erected to them and citizens were taken to an emperor's altar and told they must put a pinch of incense on it and confess Caesar as god or they would be killed. One visiting the ruins of ancient Ephesus today would be only too aware of the great temple to Vespasian, Titus, and Domitian located right beside the market place and of the temple to Trajan just down the street. Those who refused to worship the emperor were regarded as committing treason and, thus, were killed. The second beast, whom John also called the false prophet, is easily recognized as the Cult of Emperor Worship, those going about promoting worship of the emperor. Remember, this second beast comes up with the first beast, serves him, and goes down to defeat with him. So this second beast cannot represent some entity that exists long after the Roman Empire is gone.

So what will the Christians do? They can respect the ruling emperor as their political head, but they cannot worship him as a god. Satan has set up what he thinks is the perfect dilemma for Christians. Either they worship the emperor, which means renouncing their faith, or they will be subjected to horrible means of death. He thinks he has a perfect plan and that he, of course, will win. But Christians, strengthened by the message of Revelation, hold to their testimony and refuse to worship the emperor. They are, therefore, killed by the thousands. Some say as many as six million Christians were martyred during the approximately two hundred years of the Roman persecution. Others think this number is much too high. Obviously no accurate records are available, but that there was severe persecution of Christians during this time there can be no doubt. They were killed in large numbers and in the most terrible ways. Some were eaten by wild animals in front of a crowd, others were set afire, others were tied to the wheel of a chariot and driven over cobblestones until they were cut in half. Some were even crucified. This persecution began under Nero. He was the emperor who killed Paul and others. Persecution subsided under Vespasian and Titus but resumed in an even stronger form under Domitian who ruled from 81 to 96 AD. Other emperors, during the second and third centuries, continued the persecution. No doubt, this attack on Christianity was the strongest ever mounted. Yet, Satan did not get the outcome he sought. He did not scare everyone away. The persecution, in fact, helped to establish Christianity. As people saw how firmly Christians held to their faith, they wanted to know why. As Christians went out to be killed, they often were singing hymns and as they were killed, others came along to take their place. When the period of intense persecution was over, Christianity was stronger than when it began. Eventually even the Roman Emperor Constantine confessed Christ.

So chapter 13 reveals the two agents Satan will use to carry out his scheme to eliminate the church. He will bring up the Roman Empire, the strongest force on earth, to do his bidding. He will cause the Roman Empire to decide to turn its power against Christians because they will refuse to participate in a growing practice of emperor worship. When they refuse this worship, they will be regarded as traitors and will be killed. His seemingly perfect plan, however, fails to take into account that Christians will be faithful and their courage will attract others to the cause.

By the time we reach the end of chapter 13, the period of intense persecution under the beast, to last for 1260 days or 42 months, has come to an end. Satan has used his strongest weapon—and has failed in this fourth attack.

Perhaps we should say a word about 666 before passing on. In the last verse of chapter 13, the reader is encouraged to calculate the number of the beast, which is a man's number. When he does the calculation, he will find the number to be 666. We have no way of being certain how to solve this riddle and thus to use it as a clue as first century Christians could. They knew something from their culture we don't know. So what was a clue for them is not a clue for us. Since we don't know what they knew about this counting of a man's name, we can't be sure how to solve the riddle. A frequently offered suggestion is that John is using the method of letting a letter of the alphabet stand for a number. We know, for example, that in Roman numerals a "v" equals five and "x" equals ten and "c" a hundred. Some have taken the name of Caesar Nero and by such a calculation come up with 666. Since he was the first Roman Emperor to persecute Christians, this could be the meaning. We can't know for sure, but certainly many of the modern suggestions such as a big computer in Belgium, or a president of the United States, or the bar codes at the grocery store are not the answer. These would have meant nothing to the original readers and whatever the meaning was is offered as a clue to help them. So, we don't have enough information to let 666 be a clue to help us, but we have plenty of other clues to find the fundamental meaning of the book.

CHAPTER 14: THE MARTYRS AND THE ANNOUNCEMENT

In chapter 14 John sees the Lamb, Jesus, standing on Mount Zion. Says Mount Zion, means heaven. With the Lamb are the 144,000 who had the name of God written on their foreheads in chapter 7 when they were on the earth. Now they are in heaven, having been redeemed from earth. They had proven themselves faithful by not defiling themselves with women and by not lying. Thus they have been faithful to God by refusing idolatry or sexual immorality and they have not lied about their faith in Jesus. Thus, these later martyrs have joined the earlier martyrs of chapter 6. What was predicted there about more brethren being killed has now taken place. All these together, now in heaven, follow the Lamb and sing a song only they can learn. They are special.

Then comes an angel who cries with a loud voice that the hour of God's judgment has come. A second angel shouts, "Fallen! Fallen is Babylon the Great, which made all the nations drink the maddening wine of her adulteries" (14:8). And a third angel calls out that those who have worshiped the beast and his image and received his mark will drink the wine of God's fury for they shall suffer eternal punishment.

By contrast, another voice says, "Blessed are the dead who die in the Lord . . . for they shall rest from their labors" (14:13). The period of Roman persecution, the 1260 days, is now over. God will now move to bring down the persecutor. The early martyrs called for this in chapter 6, but were told to wait. That wait is over as word comes that Babylon, an appropriate code name for Rome, will fall. In Chapter 11 the 1260 day or 42 month period was described, and this was followed by the joyful announcement of the downfall of the persecutor. Here we are at the same point in the story. The period of persecution is over and the announcement of the coming fall is made. The last part of Act 1 has been repeated with more details as the beginning part of Act 2.

The fall of the persecutor is now pictured as reaping. The enemies of Christ are being cut down like grapes and put in the winepress of God's wrath to be squeezed out. This suggests, of course, their defeat. While details of that defeat remain to be given, it is powerfully announced to build the anticipation.

CHAPTER 15: THOSE VICTORIOUS OVER THE BEAST

John now sees in heaven those "who had been victorious over the beast and his image" (15:2). The beast had killed them, but they had won the victory. There are far worse things than death, even than death by horrible means. For all those who are faithful to Christ, death by whatever means is but a transport to better things. Ultimately, therefore, those who are Christ's win the victory. These martyrs sing their victory song, "Great and marvelous are your deeds, Lord God Almighty. Just and true are your ways, King of the ages" (15:3). They continue, "All nations will come and worship before you, for your righteous acts have been revealed" (15:4). As this second act is moving toward its climax, then, there is great joy and praise in heaven from those who have suffered so much for the cause of Christ. The answer to their question of "How long" is in sight.

Now out of the heavenly temple come seven angels and each is given a bowl containing a plague of God's wrath to be poured out.

CHAPTER 16: THE SEVEN BOWLS OF WRATH

A loud voice tells the angels to begin to pour out these bowls of God's wrath and, as with the seven seals and the seven trumpets, as each angel pours out his bowl, some event of the story takes place.

The first angel pours out his bowl on the land and painful and ugly sores break out on those with the mark of the beast and who worship his image. Notice against whom the plagues are directed—those who worshipped the beast! If we are correct in our identification of the beast as the Roman Empire, we can be sure against whom the wrath of God is here directed. He is telling us both that He will (1) bring down the persecuting power and (2) how He will do it. So the first bowl is poured out on *land* and worshippers of the beast break out in painful sores.

The second angel now empties his bowl on the *sea*, turning it to blood and every thing in it dies. The third angel pours his bowl of wrath on the *rivers* and they become blood. This causes an angel to see the justice in this for those who shed the blood of the saints now have to drink blood with its obviously harmful consequences. So far, something against the land, the sea, and the rivers. And note especially that the plagues are against those who persecuted Christians.

The fourth angel pours out his bowl on the *sun* and it becomes very hot and people curse the name of God and refuse to repent and glorify him. Several important points here. Again, the plagues are against evil doers. Also this cannot be an end-of-time event because at that time every knee shall bow and every tongue confess Jesus as Lord (Philippians 2:10). That these did not repent suggests that repentance was still possible. At the end of time, however, no one has the opportunity to repent. So these plagues are not end-time events. They are, rather, consequences that come on those who have persecuted God's people. But what actual consequences are symbolized?

Notice a familiar pattern? Something happens to the *land, seas, rivers, and sky*. When the first four trumpets were blown, something happened to *one-third* of the land, seas, rivers, and sky. That was, we said, to warn the persecutor. Now something happens to the *totality* of land, seas, rivers, and sky. This change in amount means a change in purpose. The *partial* destruction was for warning. The *total* destruction signifies defeat. As with the first four trumpets, God will use natural disasters, but now they will be part of His way to bring total destruction to Rome. Read any thorough history of the fall of the Roman Empire and you will note that there were many natural disasters that contributed to Rome's fall— earthquakes, floods, volcanic eruptions, fires, winds. God here is saying, I will bring down the persecutor and natural disasters will be one of the means I will use to do it.

When the fifth angel empties his bowl directly on the throne of the beast to turn it dark, this plunges the kingdom into darkness. Still they refused to repent (16:10-11). As with the locusts of the fifth trumpet, which suggested a pattern of evil against itself, here again we see a picture of the immorality and corruption of the rulers of the Empire. When the seat of power in a nation goes dark, the entire nation will soon be plunged into darkness. If the leadership is immoral, the nation is in grave danger. And so it is here. With the leadership spreading corruption, the entire kingdom is soon dark. There is a great lesson here for any nation. "Sin is a reproach to any people." Violent entertainment, high divorce rate, sexual immorality, corruption in government, pagan worship, drunkenness and debauchery, all of these were prominent in the city of Rome, the seat of power. With this fifth bowl, God is saying that the result of such behavior has now "come home to roost." The consequences due from such behavior will begin to turn the Empire into darkness. Along with natural disasters, then, God will also use the consequences of Rome's own immorality to weaken it and thus contribute to its fall. Any history of Rome will verify that Rome's own moral weakness was a factor in its fall.

The sixth angel pours his bowl on the Euphrates River to dry it up so the kings from the east, with their armies, can come across. As we saw with the parallel sixth trumpet, the Euphrates was Rome's eastern boundary and to dry that up was symbolic of saying all of Rome's borders will be vulnerable to outside attacks. And it was, indeed, the attacks of the Huns, Goths, Visigoths and Vandals, coming from beyond Rome's borders, that proved to be the major factor in Rome's fall.

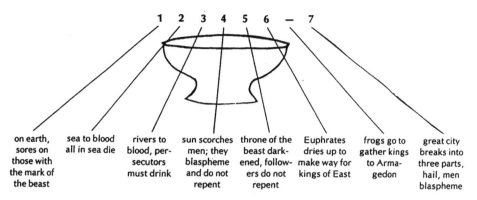

1	2	3	4	5	6	—	7
on earth, sores on those with the mark of the beast	sea to blood all in sea die	rivers to blood, persecutors must drink	sun scorches men; they blaspheme and do not repent	throne of the beast darkened, followers do not repent	Euphrates dries up to make way for kings of East	frogs go to gather kings to Armageddon	great city breaks into three parts, hail, men blaspheme

So God has now said He will bring down the persecutor and that He will do it by a combination of natural disasters, the consequences of its own corruption, and attacks from beyond its borders. First there was a period of warning through these means and, when Rome did not repent, these same methods will now be used to bring the Empire to defeat. Earlier destruction to the point of one-third and now completely.

As these powers are unleashed and begin to work their destructive power, however, we see a new development in the story (16:13-21). The dragon (Satan), the first beast (Roman Empire), and false prophet (second beast who is the Cult of Emperor Worship) see that God has set in motion the forces that can bring the Empire to defeat. They determine not to sit idly by and let this happen. They develop, therefore, a plan to rally those who are their allies, the nations that make up the Empire. The dragon and two beasts, therefore, send frogs out of their mouths to gather these kings to do battle at Armageddon.

That's what it says. What does it mean? First of all we must recognize that this is a passage filled with highly symbolic images. A dragon who is not really a dragon, meets with two beasts who are not really beasts, and they send frogs who are not really frogs out of their mouths which are not really mouths. The message the frogs carry to the subordinates is to gather at Armageddon. In the midst of all this symbolism, surely it is likely that the term Armageddon is not intended to mean war-fare at an actual place. The term "Armageddon" would translate literally into Mount of Megiddo. Megiddo is a famous site in northern Israel which was the location of a fortress to protect the Israelites from invading armies. King Solomon had a large outpost there as did King Ahab. The valley beside this hill, the Valley of Jezreel, was the site of many famous battles. It was here that Deborah and her forces defeated Sisera, that Gideon, with his three hundred, defeated the Midianites, that Saul and Jonathan were slain following their fight against the Philistines, that King Ahaziah died in battle and that King Josiah died as he fought against Egyptians. Mount Megiddo and the valley beside it, then, were famous as a great battleground. So famous, in fact, that the place can be used as a figure of speech for making a final, titanic struggle.

We all know how famous battlegrounds can be used figuratively. If we say, for example, that someone "met his Waterloo," we do not think he has gone to Belgium to the actual battlefield where Napoleon was defeated. One can meet his Waterloo and never leave home. We might also use Bunker Hill or Gettysburg as figures for important turning points. Since the word Armageddon, used only in this verse of the Bible, appears in the midst of a highly symbolic passage and since it can be taken to mean "to make a great, final stand," that is what it is intended to mean. As Satan and his forces see their powerful empire beginning to fall into defeat, they determine not to let God win without a struggle. So, they say, let's make a final stand like so many have done beside Megiddo.

Remember that at this point in Revelation the topic is not the end of the world. We are at a point in the story where the Roman Empire is being destroyed. This is how early Christians would have understood the story at this point. That we are told people are not repenting at the pouring out of the bowls is a clear indication this is not an end-of-the-world event for at the end of the world, there is no opportunity to repent. When we understand that this is part of the story of the book of Revelation about the persecution of Christians by the Roman Empire and how God is eventually going to bring that power down to defeat, we know we are not near the end of time. Also when we understand that the book of Revelation gives as its own timetable that its main story line is about things that will "happen soon" after its writing, we know this important element of the main story is not going to take place two thousand years after the book was written.

Notice, too, there is no description here of a battle. The meaning simply is that, as Satan and his two allies see their plan failing and the Empire being defeated by the power God has brought against it, they refuse to go down easily. They still want to fight and this is expressed by the their desire to "gather their forces" for a final effort as so many did in the valley near Megiddo.

Remember, too, against whom the bowls of wrath were directed—the beast and his followers. These existed in the early centuries after Christ and were prime persecutors of the early church. "Armageddon" comes after the six bowls are poured out on the Roman Empire and so must have a meaning connected with that part of the story told in Revelation.

This passage is not, then, a description of some great war just before the end of time. That does not fit the symbolic nature of the passage, does not fit the Revelation time table, does not fit the details given here of just a gathering of forces and not a great battle, and does fit the context of the subject of chapter 16.

As we come to Revelation 16:17, the seventh angel pours out his bowl into the air and from the temple of God in heaven comes a loud voice shouting, "It is done." When God chooses to bring the matter to an end, it is over and none of the "Armageddon" efforts of Satan and his allies can stop it. Lightning, thunder, and a great earthquake now strike the great city and it splits into three parts and the cities of the nations collapse. Huge hailstones also fall and the enemies of God curse Him. Again, not the end of time because no one will curse God then.

At this point we have finished the basic storyline of the book of Revelation. God has heard the question of the martyrs about "How long" and He has answered that more will die in persecution before the time comes to bring justice to the persecutor. We have seen the time of warnings, the greater persecution of the 1260 days or 42 months, and then the announcement that God was ready to move. Then came the seven bowls, indicating that God was putting the forces of Rome's final destruction into motion and nothing Satan and his allies could do would stop it. Now the city and the empire it supported have fallen and justice has been done. The book of Revelation could end here and its basic story would be complete. God desired, however, to give some additional details and to extend the story past its main thrust, and that is what follows in the final chapters.

CHAPTER 17: THE HARLOT NAMED BABYLON

Previously we have had three major figures introduced as leaders for evil: the dragon (Satan), the first beast (the Roman Empire), and the second beast or false prophet (Cult of Emperor Worship.) With the start of chapter 17, we are introduced to a fourth figure from the dark side: the harlot or prostitute. She is luxuriously clothed in purple and scarlet and jewels. She leads the kings of the world in immorality. She rides on the back of the beast. She rules over peoples, multitude, nations, and languages. And on her head is a band reading "Babylon the Great," suggesting that she is similar to the capitol city of ancient Babylon, a leader in oppressing God's people. In her hand is a cup full of the blood of those who hold the testimony of Jesus and she has drunk so much of this blood, she is intoxicated. In Revelation 17:18, the Scriptures plainly says that "the woman you saw is the great city that rules over the kings of the earth." Only one city could possibly fit all these clues and certainly that city would have come to the mind of those Christians who first received the book. Only the city of

Rome led the kings of the world in immorality. Only the city of Rome rode on the back of the Empire and reigned over all the nations. Only the city of Rome would have been so richly adorned. Only the city of Rome, in that day, could have been compared to Babylon, and only the city of Rome could have been called "that great city that rules over the kings of the earth." So, a study of all these characteristics makes it very clear as to what Christ wanted us to think of when we heard of this city.

CHAPTER 18: THE CITY NAMED BABYLON

The description of the city of Rome as an evil woman is carried through chapter 17 but when we come to chapter 18, the city is now described in terms of an actual city, but still under the name "Babylon." We are told of the great agony in the world when its capital city falls. The kings of the earth will mourn when they see her burning. The merchants will mourn because their trade opportunities are over. The musicians will no longer have a place to play and weddings will cease. The reason for all of this: "In her was found the blood of prophets and of the saints, and of all who have been killed on the earth" (18:24). So it is clear again. God is going to bring down those who have persecuted His church and their fall will be total and final.

CHAPTER 19: THE FALL OF THE HARLOT AND TWO BEASTS

Chapter 19 begins with a great multitude shouting their praise to God. Think of a stadium full of soccer fans after their team has just won a world cup victory. This multitude is composed of that great host of early martyrs of Revelation 6:9 and 7:9 and the later martyrs who were symbolically numbered 144,000. They shout Hallelujah because God has made true and just judgments. They rejoice because He has "judged the great harlot" and has "avenged on her the blood of his servants" (19:2). Remember in Revelation 6:9 when the martyrs called out for God to *judge* and to *avenge* their blood. Now He has done exactly that, just as they had asked and they scream their approval. The book of Revelation has now come full circle. The martyrs asked God to bring down the persecutor.

He said wait a while because more of the brothers and servants will have to suffer persecution. That has now taken place. He warned the persecutor but he did not repent. Then He announced that the persecutor would be destroyed and that defeat is taking place. Of the four evil characters introduced, the first to be defeated is the harlot, the city of Rome. With her fall, there is great joy and praise for God.

Next the chapter says the wedding of the Lamb has come because His bride has made herself ready. She is clothed in linen (white robes) which represent the righteous acts of the saints (19:8). We must view this wedding in light of the context of the entire book of Revelation and, in particular, of chapter 19. The topic here is not the end of time but the victory celebration over the agents of Satan who have tried to destroy the church. Because of the faithfulness of the Christians of that era, along with the help God has given them, the church survives and the enemies are going down to defeat. The righteous acts here are the faithful deeds these early Christians did in refusing to worship the beast and in continuing to proclaim their faith. At this point in the story, it is time to begin celebrating because the enemies are going down to defeat. Remember that in the verses just before those mentioning the wedding feast, the topic was the victory over the harlot. Because the church served faithfully, even giving their lives for the cause, John sees that they are now ready for this intimate relationship with Christ symbolized by the wedding supper.

John is so excited with this wonderful story that he falls at the feet of the angel who is helping reveal it to him. But the angel tells John not to worship him for he is just a fellow servant. God alone is to be worshipped.

In verse 11 we pick up again with the story of how God brings down the forces of persecution. The fall of the harlot has been told. Now the story of what happens to the two other agents of Satan is revealed. John sees a rider on a white horse whose name is Faithful and True. His eyes are like fire and he wears many crowns. His robe is dipped in blood and His name is the Word of God. Out of His mouth comes a sharp, two-edged sword with which He shall smite the nations. On His thigh and His robe are written the words "King of King and Lord of Lords."

Surely no one would fail to rec-ognize that all of these clues point to Jesus Christ. The army following Christ are the martyrs wearing their white robes. It should be said that this is not the "white horse" and rider seen in chapter 5. That rider had a bow and a single crown. He was part of a parade of horsemen all of whom were given power as they came riding across the stage pictured there. Jesus is in no way parallel to the riders there and He did not have to be given power by someone else. And in that scene, Jesus was pictured as a Lamb. It surely would be odd for Jesus to be both a Lamb opening the first seal and then to be pictured as the rider on a white horse coming forth as that seal is opened. As we reach this point of climax in the story, however, the Christ is now pictured as a warrior going forth to battle. Since His weapon is the sword coming out of His mouth, this is not physical warfare but spiritual. As He goes forth for this victory, how beautiful that the martyrs are following behind Him!

The beast and its vassal kings are gathered to fight but the beast is taken and the false prophet or second beast is taken with him. No real battle is described, for who can stand against the Son of God. Just as we read at the end of chapter 16 of the fall of the persecutor, Rome, after the pouring out of the bowls, here we read of *the same defeat* pictured in a different way. Now the rider on the white horse lays hold on the Roman Empire and the Cult of Emperor Worship and throws them into the Lake of Fire. Obviously such a description means the final end from which nothing can recover. These persecuting powers are finished and all their followers with them. Since the Roman Empire actually came to its final end about 475 A.D., that is a point in time with which we can link this point of the story.

So chapter 16 ended with the fall of Rome after the seven bowls of wrath were poured out and now chapter 19 ends at the same point in time. In chapters 17, 18, and 19, however, other details have been added and the joy in heaven over the victory has been shown. Particularly we are glad to see that the original question asked by the martyrs about "how long" has now been answered. God has used His power to "judge" and "avenge" and so has brought a just end to the one doing the persecuting. Satan failed in this massive attempt to destroy the early church and, as God knew from the beginning, the persecution actually strengthened and spread the church. Now it is stronger than when the persecution began. The fundamental storyline of Revelation has now been told—the cry for justice to the persecutor and God's answer to that plea.

Three of the four major figures for evil have now been defeated; only the dragon (Satan) is left. And so we close this portion of the book of Revelation. The key truth is emphasized again: Christ wins, Satan loses!

LESSON 5
THE THOUSAND YEARS AND AFTER

REVELATION 20

With the defeat of the harlot, beast, and false prophet in chapter 19, the main story of Revelation has been completed. The message to the Christians of Ephesus, Smyrna, Sardis, Pergamum, Thyatira, Philadelphia, and Laodicea has been given. They need to know that heavy persecution is coming from the Roman Empire as it will seek to force them into emperor worship. For them to be faithful to Christ during this time is vital so Satan's scheme to stop the church by persecution will fail. Even if they must die for their faith, it will be worth it. God will care for them and will eventually bring the persecuting power to defeat.

But Christ wanted to add an epilogue to that story which would carry the reader on to the end of time and into eternity. So we pick up in chapter 20 where chapter 19 stopped. The harlot, the beast, and the false prophet are defeated but the one who had used them as his agents, Satan, the dragon, remains. What happens to him?

REVELATION 20:1-6: THE THOUSAND YEARS

John sees an angel coming down out of heaven with a key to the Abyss and a great chain. He lays hold on the dragon, Satan, and binds him with the chain and casts him into the Abyss and locks it over him to imprison him for a thousand years. The reason this is done is "to keep him from deceiving the nations anymore until the thousand years is over" (20:3). That's what it says. What does it mean? Of course, this is still symbolism. Satan isn't really a dragon and God doesn't actually bind him with a chain and throw him into a bottomless pit. But the message He gives us through this imagery is certainly real and important. Satan is going to be restrained so he cannot "deceive the nations" anymore.

A question. Has Satan always been bound? To put this another way, has Satan always been under limits? Yes! God has never allowed him to do whatever he wants. In the book of Job, for example, God allowed Satan to do some things to Job but not others. In Matthew 12:29 Jesus said had He not first bound Satan, He could not have "entered his house" to cast out demons. So Christ had limits on Satan during His time on earth. Colossians 2:15 says that when Christ died He triumphed over "principalities and powers," meaning He won a victory over Satan, and Christ's death certainly put severe limits on him. In Revelation 12:9, Satan was cast down, defeated, and limited in that he could no longer be the accuser of the brethren. The point is that God has always held the upper hand and has limited Satan in different ways in different times.

As we come to another binding or limiting of Satan in Revelation 20, we need to realize that we should not seek to make this binding parallel to other bindings. We need to let the passage here tell us in just what way and for just what purpose Satan is bound this time. So what does the passage tell us?

THE THOUSAND YEARS AND AFTER

First we note when this binding begins. Chapter 20 starts when chapter 19 ends and chapter 19 ended with the fall of the Roman Empire. So the binding of Satan indicated here begins after Rome falls. Second, this binding is said to be for the purpose of keeping Satan from deceiving the nations anymore. What has Satan done earlier in the story? He deceived those nations collected into the Roman Empire. He got this world-wide coalition of nations to join him in trying to wipe out the church. God says, in effect, I let him do this once, but I will not let him do this again. For the duration of the thousand years, then, God will not let Satan use a world-wide empire in an attempt to persecute the church out of existence. This binding of Satan, then, is *not* the same binding that came when Jesus died on the cross and it did not start with the beginning of the Christian age. It is, rather, a limitation on Satan so he cannot do again what he has just done earlier in the story of Revelation. He can still tempt individuals to sin. He can still work against Christians and the church in some ways. He is not bound in every sense. But he is bound in that he cannot repeat what he had just tried to do in seeking to wipe out the through by persecution from a world-wide empire.

Not only is the binding of Satan said to last for a thousand year period, but during that same thousand year period, another event takes place. According to Revelation 20:4-6, while Satan is bound, "souls" are also reigning with Christ for a thousand years. Here is what the text says about this thousand-year reign. "I saw the souls of those who had been beheaded because of their testimony for Jesus and because of the word of God. They had not worshiped the beast or his image and had not received his mark on their foreheads or their hands. They came to life and reigned with Christ a thousand years" (20:4). That's what it says. What does it mean? To learn about the thousand-year reign, we must ask four basic questions of the text?

1. **Who reigns with Christ?** The text says it is those who had been beheaded (killed) because of their testimony for Jesus and because they would not worship the beast. We have seen these people before. We met them first in 6:9 where they were asking "How long?" and when they

received a white robe. Then we saw them in chapter 7 where they were wearing their white robes and serving before the throne of God. By chapter 14, they had been joined by more martyrs, the 144,000, and these all followed the Lamb and sang the song only they could sing. In chapter 15 these same martyrs were gathered around the heavenly sea where they sang the song of Moses and the Lamb and were identified as those who were "victorious over the beast." In chapter 19 they shout, "Hallelujah!" because the harlot has been judged, and then they join Christ as He rides in victory over the two beasts. These are the martyrs of the Roman persecution, beheaded for their testimony and because they would not worship the beast. These same ones seen throughout the book are now said to reign with Christ for a thousand years. The story of Revelation is their story. The book was sent to the seven churches, those about to undergo this terrible persecution, and as they passed through their fiery trial, they were killed for refusing to worship the beast. These are the heroes of the story and it is they alone whom the text says will reign with Christ for this thousand years. So, *who reigns? The martyrs of the Roman persecution.* Nothing is said in these verses about any one else reigning with Christ during this time.

    2. Why do they reign with Christ? To answer this "why" question we must look at the context. What has just happened? As chapter 19 came to an end, the Roman Empire and the Cult of Emperor Worship were thrown into the Lake of Fire. These two great enemies of the church have been defeated. Those who sought to persecute the church out of existence have failed and the church prevails. In addition, as the thousand years begins, Satan is bound so he cannot do again what he had just tried to do: destroy the church by persecution. So what would Christ and the martyrs naturally do as result of all of this? When you have won a great victory, what do you do? Celebrate! And that is exactly what the thousand-year reign is—a victory celebration when Christ and those killed because they would not worship the beast celebrate the beast's defeat. He tried to stop the church but Christ stopped him. What is the celebration like? The martyrs are with Jesus. It is a long celebration—a symbolic thousand years. It is like a resurrection because they live on and their cause survives—it is even called "the first resurrection." This does not mean a bodily resurrection but it means that this reign is a "revival" of the martyrs and a declaration that the second death, the Lake of Fire, has no power over them. The thousand-year reign, then, is a symbolic way of portraying the joy the martyrs will have when their enemy has been defeated. So, *why do they reign?* As a victory celebration!

3. Where do they reign with Christ? As we look through these verses we note that nothing is said directly about where they are. Certainly nothing is said about the reign being on earth. But there are plenty of clues to tell us where Christ and the souls are. First of all, note that those who reign with Christ are in the status of "souls." I saw the "souls" of those beheaded. Souls with no bodies do not live on earth; they live, rather, in the spirit realm. This alone would tell us that the reign is not an earthly one. These souls have been in the spirit realm ever since we first met them in 6:9 as "souls" under the altar. They were in heaven serving God in chapter 7, were in heaven with Christ in chapter 14, were in heaven praising God in chapter 15, were in heaven praising God for the destruction of the harlot in the early part of 19, and were riding with Christ in a spiritual victory over the beasts at the end of chapter 19. None of these would suggest that the "souls" physically are on earth.

But not only have the "souls" of martyrs been in heaven since chapter 6, Christ has been in heaven since chapter 5, when He came before the throne as a Lamb that had been slain. He was in heaven in chapter 14 where the martyrs followed Him and in chapter 19, where Christ rides in victory over the beast and false prophet, He achieves this by the power of His word (19:15) not by his leading an earthly military force. Another reason that this should be seen as a heavenly reign is because Christ and the martyrs sit on thrones. Revelation has told us of many thrones in heaven but the only earthly throne mentioned is the throne of the beast.

Since Christ and the souls have been in heaven since early in the book and since the context indicates that this is a victory celebration following the defeat of their enemy, the Roman Empire, this reign is a spiritual reign, not an earthly reign. The clear indication, then, is that this is a reign of souls in heaven, not a physical reign of souls on earth. So, *where is this reign?* In the spirit realm we call heaven.

4. When do they reign with Christ? Some believe this reign will take place *after* Christ returns. The context here, however, clearly suggests a time for the beginning of the reign. Since the thousand years begins with the start of chapter 20, it also begins at the point when chapter 19 ends. Thus, if we are right about chapter 19 ending with the fall of the beast, the Roman Empire, then the beginning point for the thousand year reign would be at that same time, about 475 A.D. When we realize that those who reign with Christ are the martyrs of the Roman persecution, it is obvious that their reign would begin when Rome falls. When we realize why they reign, to celebrate the victory over Rome, it is also obvious that the reign would begin at the time Rome falls.

If the reign begins with the fall of Rome, when does it end? The "thousand years," like other numbers in the book, is symbolic. The 42 months or 1260 days represented an actual time of about 200 years of Roman persecution. The number 144,000 was a number to show completeness, not an actual head count. The number seven for the number of horns and the number of eyes of the lamb is symbolic language to mean "full" or "complete." In such a book as Revelation, then, we would not expect a "thousand years" here to be a literal thousand years.

Chapter 20 also gives us good information about when the end of the thousand years comes. There in verses 11-15 we have a picture of the final judgment day when all the dead are gathered before the throne of God. While our detailed look at that will come shortly, we can use this point as a time peg to help us understand the length of the thousand years. If the final judgment comes in verse 11 and the description of the thousand years ends in verse 6, then how much time separates the end of the thousand years from the final judgment? The answer is not given in an actual years but that period is given a description. In verse 3, the text says that the time between the end of the thousand years and the resurrection at the end is only "a little time" or a "short time."

So, if only a little time, which could be a few days, a few months, or a few years, separates the end of the thousand years from the end of time, the expression "thousand years" is used as a period to fill the time from 475 A.D. to the end, except for this little time. For all practical purposes, then, the thousand years is a figurative period to describe the time, however long it is, from the victory over the Roman Empire to the end of time. During this time the martyrs enjoy the fruits of their faithfulness, being with Christ and savoring the fall of their persecutor.

Since some say the thousand-year reign *begins* when Christ returns, let's look at that option before looking at the remainder of chapter 20. In addition to what we have already seen from the passage about what the thousand year reign means, there are other passages which show that when Christ returns *He does not come to begin a reign on earth.* First, the nature of His kingdom is spiritual, not physical, as He says in John 18:36: "My kingdom is not of this world." And His many parables about the kingdom suggest that the kingdom is a reign in the hearts of people, not a physical reign over earthly territory. Jesus preached that His kingdom was "at hand" (Mark 1:15). He even declared that His kingdom would come during the lifetimes of those who were hearing Him (Mark 9:1). Acts 8:12 states that Philip went to Samaria to preach "the good news of the kingdom." It would hardly be good news if Jesus had come to establish as kingdom and had failed to do so. In Colossians 1:13, Paul says Christians were in the kingdom. In Revelation 1:9, John also said he and the Christians to whom he wrote were "partakers in the kingdom." And Revelation 12:10 says that with Christ established in heaven, the kingdom has come. To suggest that the kingdom still is not here does not fit these passages.

Perhaps the most striking passage, however, to state that Christ will not return to *start* a kingdom is 1 Corinthians 15:22-26. Here Paul writes that through Christ all will be raised from the dead. He, Himself, is the "firstfruits," that is, the first one to be raised from the dead never to die again. Then he says that those who are Christ's will be raised "at his coming." In John 6:39, 40, 44, and 54, Christ made it plain on what day those who are His will be raised: "the last day." This fits exactly with what Paul writes in 1 Corinthians 15:24 where he says that after Christ returns to raise the dead, then comes the end when he will give the kingdom back to God. Paul continues, "For he must reign until he has put all his enemies under his feet. The last enemy to be destroyed is death" (1 Corinthians 15:25-26). So, according to Paul, the order is this. Christ was raised from the dead. Later He will return and raise the dead, thus defeating His last enemy death. Then He will return the kingdom to God, for His mission is complete.

Paul's scenario here does not match the belief that Christ does not reign now but will later return to start a thousand-year reign on earth. Paul says, rather, that Christ reigns now and will reign until He returns to raise the dead on the last day. Then, having won the victory over all His enemies, He will return the kingdom to God. At His return, then, He will *end* His reign *not start* His reign (1 Corinthians 15:23-25).

So, *when is the thousand-year reign?* From after the fall of Rome until shortly before Christ's return. The text of Revelation 20 and other passages, as well, make it clear that the the reign of Christ pictured here begins with the fall of Rome, when the martyrs can begin to celebrate the victory, and lasts virtually until the end of time, separated from that event only by "a little time." That Christ will not return to start a physical kingdom is clear both from the nature of His kingdom and from what the scriptures say will happen when He returns: He gives the kingdom back to God.

Four questions then about the thousand-year reign. Who reigns? Christ and the martyrs of the Roman persecution. Why do they reign? To celebrate the great victory. Where do they reign? In heaven. When do they reign? From the fall of Rome until almost the end of time.

REVELATION 20:7-10: THE LITTLE TIME

Having explored the thousand-year period in verses 1-6, we now come to the next time period: the "little time." In verses 7-10, we are told that after the thousand years is over, Satan, who has been bound, will be released from his prison and will go out again to attempt to deceive the nations. During the thousand years God prohibited him from gathering a world-wide power to try to wipe out the church. Now that he is released from that limitation, however, he wants to begin that process again. He appears to gather a large number and they surround the camp of the saints but before they are said to do any harm, fire comes from heaven and devours them. Satan is then thrown into the Lake of Fire, where the beast and false prophet were thrown at the end of chapter 19. "There they will be tormented day and night for ever and ever" (20:10).

What shall we make of this description of the little time? We know Satan is released from the limitation he has been in. We know his intent to harm God's people has not changed. We know he wishes to attack the church again and starts a process of doing that. This description, however, does not indicate that he has any success in actually doing any harm. From the passage it would seem that before he has done any damage, God puts a stop to it by fire from heaven and then He ends any chance Satan can harm anyone by casting him into his final place of torment, the lake of fire. Jesus said in Matthew 25:41 that an "eternal fire has been prepared for the devil and his angels" and those who are condemned in judgment go there to be with them. Satan has now been sent to that "eternal fire."

There is much we do not know about the little time and it does little good to speculate. What seems clear is that Satan was held in "prison" in the Abyss, but that was not the final place God had prepared for him. To get him from that prison to the Lake of Fire, he has to first be released so he can be transferred. During this time of transfer, he shows that he has not changed his nature or his intent. He still wants to marshal the world against the church. But before he can do it harm, God sends fire and casts him into his final place of punishment.

Should we take this passage to mean that there will be a great persecution of Christians just before the end of the world? Probably not. The most common expression in Scripture about the coming of Christ is that it will come "like a thief" (2 Peter 3:10). That means no signs to warn of its coming. It will be entirely unexpected. Jesus even says in Matthew 24:42-44 that those who are His will not know when to expect the Master's return. Jesus' admonition to His disciples was, "Therefore keep watch, because you do not know the day or the hour" (Matthew 25:13). If Satan were to mount a terrible attack on the church just before the end, then that would be a sign that could tell us when Jesus was going to return but, He says, there will be no such signs.

So, much about the little time we don't know, and we should not speculate beyond what the text says.

REVELATION 20:11-15: THE JUDGMENT

Now we come to the third time period in chapter 20: verses 11 through 15. Satan has just gone down to his final defeat, being thrown into the Lake of Fire. Then, John says, he saw a great, white throne and the one sitting on it. And he says he saw all of the dead, the great and the small, standing before the throne. The sea gave up her dead, and death and Hades gave up their dead. This clearly suggests that all the dead, from all periods of time and both good and bad, are before God's judgment throne. Then, John says, books were opened which contained the record of what all the people had done while they were alive and they will be judged by these deeds (20:13). That brings fear to my heart to think that all that I have ever said or thought or done could be "displayed on that great video screen in the sky" for all to see and to be the basis of God's judgment for me. We have all sinned (Romans 3:23) and none of us could be approved in a judgment based on our deeds. No one! And most of those standing before God's throne will be sent to the Lake of Fire to be with Satan and all the wicked throughout eternity (Revelation 20:15 and Matthew 7:13-14). Of course, we understand that the "Lake of Fire" is a symbolic way of describing this horrible place of punishment. Says a lake of burning sulfur; means a more painful existence than we can imagine. No worse fate is possible. Sounds pretty grim, doesn't it?

But there is another book—the book of life. And if anyone's name is written in the book of life, that person will escape this terrible outcome and will not go to the Lake of Fire. Jesus gave us a way out! Someday the only thing that will matter is whether my name is written in the book of life. My money, my house, my car, my fame, my position, my success, none of this will matter at all. The *only thing that will matter* is whether my name is written in the book of life. But what must I do to have my name written in the book of life?

The concept of the book of life appears throughout Scripture. As far back as Exodus 32:33 God was keeping a list of those who were His and in that passage God threatens to blot some out of the book. In Psalm 69:28, David speaks of some being blotted out of God's book. In Luke 10:20, Jesus told His disciples to rejoice that their names were written in heaven. In Philippians 4:3, Paul speaks of his fellow workers whose names are in the book of life. Hebrews 12:23 speaks of the church of the firstborn, whose names are written in heaven. And in Revelation 3:5, Christ promised not to blot the names of Christians out of the book of life *if* they will be faithful to Him.

So, God has been making a list, checking it twice. "Gonna find out whose naughty and nice." Well, that's not an exact quotation, but it expresses the idea. He's keeping a record of who has been faithful to Him. God has always known those who were His—in Old Testament times and New. Everyone who has ever lived, then, is in one of three conditions related to this book.

1. They have *never been written in it* because they have never done what God has asked them to do. For the Christian age, this means that we must believe in Jesus and accept Him as our savior. Jesus said that only by coming to Him can we find our way to God (John 14:16; John 3:16; John 8:24; Acts 4:12). When those who believed Peter's sermon about Jesus' being the Messiah asked what more they should do, Peter told them "Repent and be baptized, every one of you, in the name of Jesus Christ, for the forgiveness of your sins" (Acts 2:38). Paul also said that believers were to be "baptized into Christ" (Galatians 3:27). Being "in

Christ" would mean that one has been added to the list of the saved. There is controversy in some quarters about whether it is necessary to be baptized before one's sins are forgiven. There is no controversy, however, whether one who repents and is baptized for forgiveness of sins has done what the Peter said would bring one into Christ. So some have not submitted to Christ and thus have no basis to expect their names to be written in the book of life.

2. Some have had their names written in the book of life but then have gone astray and *have been blotted out*. As we look at the passages that mention the book of life, many of them speak of being blotted out. Surely such statements would not appear if being blotted out were impossible. 1 John 1:6-10 is a great passage about this. It says that if Christians "walk in the light," then we have fellowship with each other and the blood of Jesus keeps on cleansing us from our sins. If, however, we claim fellowship with Christ and walk in the darkness, we lie and do not live by the truth (1 John 1:6). So having started down the pathway with Christ, if we keep on walking in the light, seeking to do what is right and correcting sins as we are aware of them, He keeps on cleansing us. But if we leave the road of light to walk in the darkness, then He no longer takes our sins away. We do not, of course, leave the road of light every time we sin. As the passage says, we walk in the light and His blood keeps on cleansing us. But if we sin and no longer care, no longer try not to sin, sin and make no effort to correct it or to confess it, then we have left the light for the darkness. When we reach such a condition as this, we would be blotted out of the book of life. One who has left the light for the darkness may return if he repents and confesses and prays for forgiveness (Acts 8:20-24; Galatians 6:1).

3. The third possible condition, is that one has been written in the book of life and is *still listed there*. This one has believed in Christ, repented of his sins and obeyed Christ in baptism so God will add him to the body of Christ (Mark 16:16; Acts 2:38, 47). Those who are written in the book and remain faithful to Christ will continue to be in the book until the time of judgment.

Each of us should ask, "Is my name in the book of life at this moment?" If the answer to that is "No" or "I'm not sure," then we should take immediate steps to use the grace Christ offers for us to be in His book.

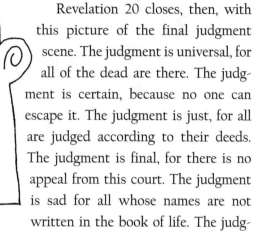

Revelation 20 closes, then, with this picture of the final judgment scene. The judgment is universal, for all of the dead are there. The judgment is certain, because no one can escape it. The judgment is just, for all are judged according to their deeds. The judgment is final, for there is no appeal from this court. The judgment is sad for all whose names are not written in the book of life. The judgment is happy for those whose names are in the book of life.

Let's all think clearly about whether we are, at this moment, in the Lamb's Book of Life and, if not, we must accept the grace of God by faith and obedience so God can add us to His list as He wants to do.

LESSON 6
THE NEW JERUSALEM

REVELATION 21 AND 22

In the last few verses of Revelation, chapter 20, we saw a picture of the judgment scene. God is on the throne with all the dead gathered before Him. Those judged on the basis of their deeds, who have not done what God has asked to have their names in the book of life, are condemned to eternal punishment. They go into the Lake of Fire, a figurative expression for final torment. Those, however, whose names are written in the book of life, have a different destiny. They will live in the New Jerusalem, the holy city. Revelation 21 and 22 give a description of the great blessings they will enjoy.

So we come now to study these last two chapters. John says, "I saw a new heaven and a new earth, for the first heaven and the first earth had passed away" (21:1). John says he "saw the new Jerusalem, coming down out of heaven from God, prepared as a bride dressed for her husband." (21:2). This verse says the city is prepared and ready, prepared like a bride who gets ready for her husband. All of us have probably been involved in some way in the preparation a bride makes for the wedding and for her husband. Jesus said, "I go to prepare a place for you" (John 14:2), and now that wonderful preparation has been made. It is ready. Why does the city "come down?" This city is part of the new heaven and new earth scene and comes "down" in the sense that it comes into John's view. God wants him to see it so he can provide a description of it for us.

In this vision, a loud voice from God's throne says, "Now the dwelling of God is with men, and he will live with them. They will be his people, and God himself will be with them and be their God. He will wipe every tear from their eyes. There will be no more death or mourning or crying or pain, for the old order of things has passed away" (21:3-4). This is the quick summation of the beautiful existence those experience who live in the city. For them, nothing bad ever happens. They enjoy eternal life in the presence of God. That alone would be sufficient description, but there is more.

This great reward is available to all, for God says, "To him who is thirsty I will give to drink without cost from the spring of the water of life. He who overcomes will inherit all this, and I will be his God and he will be my son" (21:6, 7). There is our word "overcome" again—a frequent word in Revelation. Heaven is only for "overcomers," for those who have made the effort to love, obey, serve, and honor God. As the old spiritual says, "You can't get to heaven in a rocking chair; you rock, and rock, and you stay right there." We can't earn any of our way to heaven, but, at the same time, we cannot get to heaven without making the effort God asks of us. He wants us to try. He will make allowances for our failures, but He will not reward us unless we make an effort. We must have the heart of "overcomers."

The voice from the throne of God continues and tells us who will *not* be in heaven. "But the cowardly, the unbelieving, the vile, the murderers, the sexually immoral, those who practice magic arts, the idolaters and all liars—their place will be in the fiery lake of burning sulfur" (21:8). Those who engage in such sins will go into the Lake of Fire. Notice how many of these sins would be connected with the Roman persecution. The persecutor was a murderer, sexually immoral, practiced magical arts, and was an idolater. Christians who gave in were cowardly, unbelieving, and liars. The list is not limited to such circumstances, but it does show a connection. Those who continue to live in such immoral ways should know they have no expectation of escaping the torment of hell.

Now an angel comes and says he will show John the bride, the wife of the Lamb. John then begins to describe both the city and the people who live in it. His descriptions, as we would expect in Revelation, use figures of speech. First John describes the physical appearance of the city and then he tells of the people who inhabit it. As this description comes to an end, Christ welcomes "those who wash their robes, that they may have the right to the tree of life and may go through the gates into the city."

So let's learn from John's description what it will be like for those who live in the New Jerusalem. The city shines with the brilliance of the glory of God. It is a perfect cube in shape, fifteen hundred miles wide, high and deep. The red wall, made of jasper stone, is 210 feet high, and has three openings on each of its four sides.

At each gate is one huge pearl, large enough to fill the opening and these gates, each inscribed with the name of one of the twelve tribes, are always standing open. Underneath the wall are twelve foundation layers, each made of a beautiful precious stone and on each of the foundations is written the name of one of the twelve apostles. The streets are pure gold, so pure it is transparent. John says there is no temple in the city because the Lord God Almighty and the Lamb are its temple. The Jewish temple had the holy of holies to "represent" the presence of God with His people. No such representation is needed here for God is actually with His people who shall "see His face" (22:4). There is also no need for the sun or moon because the presence of God and of Christ will give all the light that is needed. Leaders and people from all nations are there and nothing impure, or shameful, or deceitful will enter—only those whose names have been written in the Lamb's book of life.

From the throne of God flows a beautiful river of the water of life, and on each side of the river are "tree of life" trees. These yield a different crop of fruit each month and its leaves are for the healing of the nations. The curse which came on man after sin entered the world (Genesis 3) is gone and God's people will serve Him and reign with Him for ever and ever.

This is what it says. What does it mean? We must remember that we are still in a book of symbols and must look not only at the beautiful picture, but at what God wants us to learn from the picture. The most important message, of course, is that it is infinitely better to spend eternity in the New Jerusalem than in the Lake of Fire. No question about that! These two possible eternal destinies are put in stark contrast. The lake of burning sulfur pictures to us the most unpleasant experience we can imagine, multiplied many times over. We might imagine what it would be like to be thrown in something that would burn us for a short time, but to imagine living eternally in such pain is beyond our comprehension.

The same impossibility exists when we look the other direction, at the New Jerusalem. The beautiful picture God has given us of this brilliant cube, with streets of gold and the beautiful stream with tree of life fruit abundantly available and with its redeemed people from all ages and all nations is beyond our capacity to imagine. Perhaps the best word to describe what He wants us to learn from this picture is the word "perfect." Heaven will be perfect in every way.

Those who have written to help us understand this figurative picture of heaven, often present the picture like this. First, heaven will provide *perfect protection*. Its shape as a perfect cube suggests that it is impenetrable, and its high wall means that no one can enter to harm us. The twelve layers of foundation indicate that the city can never be shaken. It is so safe, in fact, that its gates always remain open. To those early Christians who were so vulnerable to attack and seemingly defenseless against the Roman soldiers, this would have been a very meaningful image. Perfect protection! Nothing can ever harm us there.

A second lesson from the description is that heaven will be a place of *perfect provision*. Notice all the things we will have in abundance. God and the Lamb will be the light and there shall be no night. We walk on streets of gold, eat of the tree of life, drink from the river of life, and bask eternally in the presence of God. Every need we have will be fully supplied. All needs totally supplied in a place whose beauty is beyond our comprehension. No need we can imagine is beyond God's power to provide! Perfect provisions!

The third concept of perfection we shall enjoy in heaven is *perfect fellowship*. The highest level of the perfect fellowship is to be eternally with the Father, the Son, and the Holy Spirit. "The dwelling of God will be with men, and he will live with them" (21:3). The intimacy with God will be so great that we shall see His face (22:4). In addition we will be with angels and with the redeemed of all ages. Imagine conversing with David, Isaiah, Peter, and Paul. I was excited to be on Mars Hill in Athens were Paul had delivered a speech two thousand years earlier. Imagine seeing him in person! And we shall, I believe, be with those we have loved and with whom we shall share the heavenly experience. On the Mount of Transfiguration, Moses was still Moses and Elijah was still Elijah, centuries after they had died. They did not lose their personal identity. When David's child died, He was consoled by the fact that "He shall not come to me, but I shall go to him" (2 Samuel 12:23). Some wonder about our knowing each other because we would then know that some loved one was not with us in heaven and that would make us sad. God has not revealed to us how He will deal with such matters but the evidence seems clear on two points: we will always be the same person we have been and God will have a way to remove all problems from heaven. So I encourage you to look forward to being with those loved ones who have gone before us and who will come after us.

The final element of perfection is that heaven will provide *perfect joy*. Not one thing can ever come along to bring any sadness to our lives. There will be no death and so no need for the sadness of separation it causes. There will be no sickness or disease to make us infirm or bring pain. There will be no growing older or losing our capacities. When the Scripture says "God shall wipe away every tear from their eyes" (21:4) it does not mean we shall have tears and God will console us. It means there will never be anything to cry about. And we shall have opportunities to serve God for "His servants will serve him" (22:3) and that service shall bring immense joy and satisfaction. Imagine a place where all the bad things have been totally removed and all the good things are multiplied a million times over. Because of our finite minds and limited experience, we cannot conceive of the smallest fraction of the good things God has in store for His children.

So, the great contrast! Far beyond the worst we can imagine on one side and far beyond the best we can imagine on the other. What will determine in which place we spend eternity? We must overcome (21:7). Whosoever will may come, but he must answer the call to come (22:17). "Whoever is thirsty" may come. If you want to go to heaven even worse than you would want a cool drink of water on a hot day, you can come (22:17). Those who "wash their robes" in the blood of the Lamb (22:14) will be prepared for heaven because they have accessed the grace provided by obeying what God has asked us to do. "Whoever wishes, let him take the free gift of the water of life" (22:17). Whoever will may come. All ages, all races, all levels of education, rich or poor, famous or unknown, slave or free, of any century—all may come to Christ if we come on His terms.

So the book of Revelation closes by placing the matter squarely before each of us. Which eternal destiny shall we choose? Will we reject Jesus and His way of life and thus place ourselves on the broad road that leads to destruction? Or will we accept Jesus and obey Him and be on the narrow road that leads to life? The amazing thing is that since Christ gave His life for us, the choice is now ours. If a million dollars were placed before you and you were told it was yours if you would meet a few provisions that were easily within your reach, you would certainly do it. God has placed before us far more than that, eternal life in a perfect place. Will you meet those provisions announced by Christ and His apostles? Will you believe in Jesus and confess that faith openly before others, will you change direction by repenting of your sins and seeking to live a faithful life with Jesus? Will you submit to baptism by immersion for the forgiveness of sins? (See these passages: Mark 16:16; Acts 2:38; Galatians 3:26-27; Acts 22:16; Romans 10:10; Romans 6:4.) Will you continue to live a life of faithfulness before Him?

The great message of Revelation is that God loves and cares for His children. As He saw terrible persecution coming, He sent a letter of assurance and comfort to those Christians about to experience the terrors of the Romans. He did not immediately remove the source of their suffering because it would eventually bring the message of Christ to more people than if there had been no persecution. So, as is so often the case, Satan meant it for evil, but God turned it into good. He sent Revelation to give His church insight into the problem and courage to face it. Because Christians by the thousands and maybe even by the hundreds of thousands or millions, were faithful unto death, we still have access to the message about Christ and His church today. Now it is our turn. We must also be faithful—by living for Christ or by dying for Him, whatever we may be called on to do.

Surely the primary lesson we can learn from Revelation, even if we do not understand every detail, is that *Christ wins and Satan loses*. We can be on the winning side if we choose to do so. The words of an old hymn express how the faith of the early Christians strengthened them for what they faced and that we should demonstrate that same faith in our lives.

O for a faith that will not shrink, though pressed by every foe,
That will not tremble on the brink of any earthly woe.
That will not murmur or complain beneath the chastening rod,
But in the hour of grief or pain, will lean upon its God.
A faith that shines more bright and clear when tempests rage without;
That when in danger knows no fear, in darkness feels no doubt.
Lord, give us such a faith as this; and then, what-e're may come,
We'll taste e'en here the hallowed bliss of an eternal home.
—William Bathhurst (1831)

Let me close this message about the wonderful book of Revelation with a story from our day. Likely you have read books by Dr. James Dobson and heard his radio program. He has many good things to say about parenting and Christian living. While we wouldn't agree on all religious matters, I believe he has helped many to live better lives.

Dr. Dobson tells story of how he asked Pete Maravich to be on his radio program. Pete still holds the record for the most points in a collegiate basketball career and had just retired from ten years with the Utah Jazz. Pete was a believer in Jesus and Dr. Dobson thought it would be great to have him on his radio broadcast. So on January 5th, 1988, Pete was in California to tape the broadcast. While he was there, the group thought it would be great fun to play a little basketball and so were on the court when suddenly Pete fell to the floor gravely ill. Before the paramedics arrived, he was dead in Dr. Dobson's arms. A heart attack at age 40 had taken one of America's great athletes.

As we all could imagine, this event caused Dr. Dobson and his family to have serious discussions about life and death and their goals. As a family they agreed their primary aim would be to live here so they could, as a family, be together in heaven. And they worked out a "shorthand" way of expressing that to each other. They would extend their hand with the thumb up and say "Be There."

Only a few months later, Dr. Dobson himself had a heart attack. He was in intensive care, hooked up to the machines, with a tube down his throat so he couldn't speak, but mentally alert. His son, nearly twenty, came to the room to see him. How do you suppose they communicated? They held out their hands, thumbs up, to say to each other, "Whatever happens here, we want to be together there."

This story has become an important part of my family life. I have told it to my children and grandchildren. And we, too, have made it our family goal. My wife has sewn cross-stitched plaques with the words "Be There" on them for all our children and married grandchildren so these words can be prominently displayed in our homes. My favorite picture is my ten grandchildren giving me the "Be There" sign. We all have key chains that say "Be There." My children gave me a license tag that reads "Be There."

We have found this to be a wonderful way to say to each other and to all we know that our goal is to "Be There." There is no better way to conclude a study of the book of Revelation than for us all to pledge to be with each other in heaven. The book closes with the beautiful picture of that perfect place. Let us all determine that we will read carefully in Scripture to learn of God's grace and what He asks us to do to access it.

Then we can all "Be There."

TEACHING
OUTLINES

LESSON 1
CLASS SESSIONS 1 AND 2

GENERAL SUGGESTIONS FOR THE TEACHER

1. Make a book available to each student or couple at the first class meeting. Give the students an assignment to read the pages in the book you plan to cover at the next class meeting.

2. Involve students as much as possible. Use a question-answer format and let the class discuss certain issues. In the teaching outlines, questions are suggested to help you use the question/answer style. Sometimes an answer is provided in parentheses after the question, but usually you will need to get the answer from the parallel place in the chapter you are discussing.

3. Develop a weekly quiz with multiple-choice, fill in the blank, and matching questions, or ask for a list of items. The test (you may call it a "written review" to make it sound less scary) can cover both the reading assigned and the previous class session. To save class time, have the quiz available for students who wish to take it as they enter the classroom. Ask them to fill it out in the time before the class session actually begins, and early in the class give the answers and let each student grade his/her own paper.

4. The objectives of this class are that the student can:

    A. List the five major approaches suggested for the book of Revelation.

    B. List and explain the seven key factors that enable us to determine which of these approaches is most in harmony with the book of Revelation.

    C. Identify who or what is represented by the major symbols in Revelation.

    D. Tell the basic storyline of Revelation.

    E. Express a willingness to be faithful as the early Christians were and to share in the same hope they did.

5.   Many songs are based on Revelation or echo its message. Use one of these in each session as a way of helping the class understand both the songs and the book. Make a list of songs like: "Victory in Jesus," "Worthy is the Lamb," "Worthy Art Thou," "On Zion's Glorious Summit," "In the Land of Fadeless Day," "There is a Habitation," "There's a Great Day Coming," "Faith of our Fathers," and many, many more. Ask the class to be expanding this list of songs.

TEACHING CLASS SESSION 1

1.   Introduce visitors and have a song and prayer.

2.   **Q**: What first comes to mind when you think of studying Revelation? (Take just a few answers.)

3.   We know there are different views about the meaning of the book of Revelation. One of our objectives is to discover what the book meant to those who first received it and, from that, to ask what message Christ wants us to learn today. Five views of the book are the most prevalent. Let's first review these five and then seek to determine which of them is most in harmony with the book itself and, thus, most likely how early Christians understood it.

   A.   Revelation was written near the end of the first century A.D. primarily to help Christians of the late first century and next two centuries deal with the persecution from the Roman Empire. Christ wanted to assure them that, if they will be faithful, Christ will punish the Empire and reward the Christians. **Q**: How many have heard of this view? **Q**: Who is an author that takes this view?

   B.   Revelation is primarily about the coming fall of Jerusalem. Thus, the book was written in the early 60's A.D. and is to help Christians be ready for this important event. **Q**: How many have heard of this view? **Q**: Who is an author that takes this view?

C.   Revelation is given to predict major religious and political events in world history between the first and second comings of Christ. Thus, it speaks of Roman Emperors, the Roman Catholic Church, Mohammed, John Calvin, Martin Luther, France, England, and other historical people and events. **Q**: How many have heard of this view? **Q**: Who is an author that takes this view?

D.   Revelation is not about *specific* events in history at all. It presents, rather, a general cycle of events (or principles) that repeats over and over: wherever Christ is preached, religious and political opposition will follow. Christians should understand this cycle and be prepared to deal with it. Thus, Revelation is *equally* about every age and place where the gospel is preached. **Q**: How many have heard of this view? **Q**: Who is an author that takes this view?

E.   Revelation is focused on events near the end of the world. According to this view, we now live in chapter 3. There will soon be a rapture, a great battle over Israel climaxing in Armageddon, and then Christ returns to start a thousand-year kingdom, reigning over the world from Jerusalem. **Q**: How many have heard of this view? **Q**: Who is an author that takes this view?

We shall seek to discover which of these views is most likely the one Christ intended for Christians who first received the book. Seven keys from the book can help us. We will start looking at these today and finish them up next week, and then we will seek to use these to identify the view most likely to be the one intended.

4.   Here are seven key points from Revelation which we should understand as we start our study. We'll cover some today and others in our next class meeting.

A.   Revelation is written in symbols.

     i.   **Q**: Should we take the Bible literally or figuratively?

         a.   Like all language, the Bible uses both. **Q**: What are some figures Jesus uses to teach about Himself?

         b.   How do we tell whether something is literal or figurative? We usually assume something is literal unless a literal view is clearly not the meaning. Jesus is obviously not really water or bread or light. So in these cases we take the figurative view.

     ii.   Revelation uses many figures not intended to be taken literally.

         a.   **Q**: What are some of the figures used in Revelation?

         b.   We will study these as we go through the book. The point for now is that Revelation makes extensive use of figures, far more than any other New Testament book, and knowing this will help us understand it. These figures are a kind of "code," and as we seek to understand what Revelation means, knowing it is in "code" will help us decide which view to take.

B.   Revelation will "shortly come to pass."

     i.   Let's read some of the verses that speak of this. (See Chapter 1.)

     ii.   **Q**: What would those first receiving the book understand from these statements? **Q**: What does Jesus mean by saying I come "quickly"?

     iii.   The book of Revelation, then, provides a timetable for its major events. They will happen relatively soon after the book is written. The story of Revelation will take some years to unfold, but its focus is clearly on events that will "shortly come to pass."

C.   Revelation was given to comfort persecuted Christians.

    i.   Let's read some of the verses that speak of this.

    ii.   **Q**: What would those who first received the book understand from these comments about persecution? **Q**: Where were the churches to whom the book of Revelation was directed? **Q**: What was the source of persecution to which these people were subjected between 100 and 300 A.D.? **Q**: How severe was this persecution? **Q**: What was its final outcome?

5.   Before the next class meeting, be sure to read all of Lesson 1 in your book. (If you plan to give a quiz, be sure to tell people about it and generally what questions to expect.)

TEACHING CLASS SESSION 2

1.   Use a test as indicated above and give the answers or do a little oral review on the previous lesson. Be sure to review key points from previous lessons as you begin each lesson. Have a song connected with Revelation and a prayer at the beginning of class and introduce any visitors.

2.   Continue the study of the seven keys. Review the three keys covered in the previous lesson. We pick up with the fourth key.

    A.   Revelation Identifies the Dragon and Two Beasts.

        i.   The book of Revelation is like a play, so to understand it we must know who is in the cast of characters. Three of them are a dragon and two beasts. Let's see what these symbols represent.

        ii.   From Revelation 12:3-5, describe the dragon. Let some read Revelation 12:9 and others Revelation 20:2. **Q**: Who is the dragon?

        iii.   The first beast is introduced in Revelation 13:1-7. As we read this, make a list of his characteristics. Add to this what Revelation 17:9-10 says. **Q**: What entity would fit all these characteristics? So the beast represents the Roman Empire and his heads represent its emperors.

    iv.   The second beast is introduced in Revelation 13:11-17. As we read this, make a list of his characteristics. **Q**: From his qualities, what is this beast's identity? **Q**: What would the early Christians see in this figure? (Those encouraging worship of the Roman Emperors and even forcing people to worship them: The Cult of Emperor Worship.)

    v.   So we have identified three major characters in the story: the dragon, the first beast, the second beast. **Q**: What does each of these represent?

B.   Revelation Identifies the Harlot whose name is Babylon.

    i.   Read Revelation 17:1-7, 15-17. As you read these verses, make a list of the characteristics of the harlot. **Q**: What would Christians of the late first century and years following have connected with these characteristics? **Q**: What is her connection with the first beast?

    ii.   **Q**: Why is the name "Babylon" appropriate for such an entity?

C.   Revelation Identifies the 1260 Days.

    i.   Read Revelation 11:2-7, 12:6, 14 and 13:7. **Q**: In what different lengths is the period described? **Q**: Are these all the same length?

    ii.   What type of activity is said to occur in this period?

    iii.   Who is in charge of this persecution?

    iv.   Do these references mean a literal three and a half years?

    v.   When was the Roman persecution? (From about 65 A.D., off and on, until Constantine's edict in 313

A.D.) As with animals, time periods in Revelation are also to be taken in a figurative sense.

    D.   Revelation Identifies the Kingdom.

        i.   Read Revelation 1:6 and 1:9. **Q**: What do we learn about God's kingdom? (A kingdom of priests and so a spiritual kingdom. John was in it, so it existed then. The Christians John wrote were also in it.)

        ii.   So the kingdom of Revelation is a spiritual kingdom existing in the first century of which Christians were a part. See John 18:36 and Col. 1:13.

3.   We have now covered the seven keys. Based on what we have learned from these keys, which of the five views of Revelation is the most likely the view of those who first received the book?

    A.   **Q**: How does what we have learned fit the "future time" view? **Q**: Does this view fit "soon"? **Q**: Does this view fit "written in symbols"? **Q**: Does this view fit the purpose of helping persecuted saints of the early church? **Q**: Does this view give the proper meaning of the two beasts? **Q**: Does this view give the right meaning to the kingdom?

    B.   **Q**: How does what we have learned fit the "philosophical" view? Of course there are lessons in the book for all time. **Q**: But does the book speak of a particular set of circumstances in which early Christians found themselves? **Q**: Is the persecution of Revelation under a particular enemy of the church? **Q**: How does this view fit "soon"?

    C.   **Q**: How does what we have learned fit the "foretells history" view? Of course, Revelation foretells some history. **Q**: But is it a prediction of the major events of the entire Christian age? **Q**: Fit "soon"? **Q**: Fit persecution? **Q**: Fit the correct meaning of first and second beast? **Q**: Fit Harlot? **Q**: Comfort early Christians?

    D.   **Q**: How does what we have learned fit the "fall of Jerusalem" view? Requires the date of writing to be earlier than the best evidence would indicate. The time of writing was more likely near the end of the first century. **Q**: To people in what geographic area was the book addressed? If the book is primarily about the fall of Jerusalem, why address the book to churches in Asia instead of Christians in Jerusalem? This view makes the harlot to be Jerusalem. **Q**: How well does that fit?

E.　　**Q**: How does what we have learned fit the "fall of Rome" view? **Q**: Fit soon? **Q**: Fit the identity of the beasts and harlot? **Q**: Comfort persecuted Christians? **Q**: Fit 1260 days? **Q**: Fit what we know of the history of the early church and its persecution?

4.　　Review. Close your books. **Q**: So who is really behind the coming persecution? (Satan) What is his aim? (To destroy the church) Who will be his agent in the persecution? (Roman Empire) Why will the Empire oppose the church? (They will refuse to worship the Emperor) What dilemma will Christians face? (To worship and leave the faith or not to worship and be killed) Thus, no Christians will be left. To combat this very threat, Christ sends the book of Revelation. It is encouragement for those early Christians to "be faithful unto death" so He can give them the crown of life. We, likewise, must have this same devotion to the cause of Christ. The book says Christ will win and Satan will lose. **Q**: What persecution should we be prepared for?

5.　　Assignment: Read for the next Class Session the first half of Lesson 2 in the book. Also read Chapters 2 and 3 in Revelation. Prepare for the quiz.

LESSON 2
CLASS SESSIONS 3 AND 4

TEXT: REVELATION 1-3

Class Sessions 3 and 4 are based on Lesson 2 of the book which covers Revelation 1-3. Revelation 1 gives some background for the book. Revelation 2 and 3 contain seven letters from Christ to seven churches in cities of Asia Minor, where Emperor Worship was a very important thing and where churches needed to be strengthened and prepared for what was coming upon them.

TEACHING CLASS SESSION 3
TEXT: REVELATION 1

1.   Introduce visitors and new members. Start with a song based on Revelation and ask the class for the connecting points. Pray for those in your class who have special needs. Review the answers to the quiz and let the class demonstrate through oral answers what they remember from the past lesson.

2.   Ask the class to close their class books and turn to Revelation 1 and from it answer the following questions.

3.   Q: What does chapter 1 of Revelation teach us about the one who wrote the book? (John on Patmos. Most take this to be the apostle of John, now in old age.)

Q: Why is he on Patmos? (Verse 9— I am a "companion with you in the tribulation." He was exiled there "because of the word of God and the testimony of Jesus." Those in authority wanted to put him where he couldn't continue to be a witness for Christ.)

Q: From whom does the message really come? (Verse 1.)

Q: Describe the figure who appears to John.

Q: What characteristics of this figure help us to identify Him? (First and last, living one, dead and now alive, keys of death and hades, etc.) **Q**: Who is this figure? (Risen Christ.) **Q**: What does he tell John to do? (Write what he sees and hears and send it to seven churches.) **Q**: Where are the churches located? (Asia Minor, now Turkey.) **Q**: Where is Patmos located? (In the Agean Sea.)

4.   Now let's look briefly at the contents of the seven letters (today and next class).

Notice that each letter follows about the same pattern. (1) Greetings to the church (from one whose identity is revealed by symbols); (2) commendations to the church; (3) weaknesses of the church; and (4) promises to the church. Our study in this lesson and the next will discuss seven principles which appear in several of the letters. If Christ were writing this congregation, He would probably mention most of these.

5.   Principle No. 1. *Christ Knows Every Christian.* Notice that most letters have this statement, "I know your ...." Christ knows us well, too. **Q**: In what situations are you glad Christ knows you? **Q**: What might we do differently if we stopped to think Christ is watching us?

6.   Principle No. 2. *Christ Wants Churches to Guard Their Teaching.* Have students read some or all of the following verses: 2:2; 2:14; 2:20; 3:3; and 3:8. (You may want to write the verses to be read on cards and hand them out before class so someone will be ready to read. This is also a way to involve more in the class.) **Q**: How does Christ describe the message He wants them to follow? (What you have heard, my word.) Did Christ's churches always follow this admonition? (No and hence the departure from the faith which Paul predicted in 1 Tim. 4:1-4; and 2 Tim. 4:1-4; and Acts 20:30.) **Q**: Do we need the same admonition today? **Q**: What are some of the forces that might lead us away from His Word?

7.   Give a brief review of the lesson today and encourage the class to read Revelation 2 and 3 again to prepare for the next class.

TEACHING CLASS SESSION 4
TEXT: REVELATION 2-3

1. Introduce visitors, sing a song based on Revelation, and pray for us to learn to be better Christians and this congregation to be better because we have studied these letters from Christ to His churches. Review the last lesson and check the quiz. Have the class close their books and open their Bibles and have some ready to read verses you want read.

2. Principle No. 3. *Christ Wants Christians to Grow in Service.* Have someone read Rev. 2:19. **Q**: What did Jesus think of the level of service in Thyatira? (Getting better and better.) Read Rev. 3:8. **Q**: What did Jesus offer this church? (To set before it open doors of opportunity.) **Q**: Would Christ think we have open doors before us? **Q**: What are some of them? Read Rev. 2:4-5. **Q**: What did Christ think of the level of service in Ephesus? (Not loving as much and consequently not serving as well.) **Q**: Does this description fit this congregation? Read Rev. 3:15. **Q**: To what does Christ compare the church of Laodicea? **Q**: What other words does He use to characterize this church? Read Rev. 3:1. **Q**: How does Christ describe the level of work in Sardis?

    Christ describes the level of service in five different churches in five different ways. **Q**: Which of these descriptions best fits our congregation? **Q**: Is our trend toward more and better service or is it going the other way? **Q**: What percentage of our congregation could we say is at work for the Lord?

3. Principle No. 4. *Christ Wants Christians to Live Pure Lives.* Look at the letters to Thyatira (2:20) and Sardis (2:14). **Q**: What immoral practices does He say are going on there? (Eating meat offered to idols and committing fornication.) **Q**: Why are Christians in these places being caught up in this type of activity? **Q**: What is the warning here for us? (Do not follow the leaders in our culture when they practice immorality. Because "everybody is doing it" does not make it right.)

4. Principle No. 5. *Christ Wants Christians to Be Ready for Persecution.* This is the main thrust of this book. **Q:** What persecution were these Christians facing? **Q:** How might this affect their lives? **Q:** In what ways do we face persecution? **Q:** How can we best prepare to meet this persecution?

5. Principle No. 6. *Christ Wants Christians to Know They Can Be Lost.* Have someone read the following verses: 2:4-5; 2:10 last sentence; 2:16; 2:20-23; 3:3; 3:18-19. **Q:** Do these verses suggest that a Christian can or cannot sin so as to be lost? (Many of these verses call for repentance or else Christ will take away their chance of heaven. See also 2 Peter 2:4; 20-22. Christ does not want us to live in fear that we will lose salvation, but neither does He want us to fall away and be lost.)

6. Principle No. 7. *Christ Wants Christians to Hope for Great Rewards.* Have someone read each of the following passages, which come at the end of each of the seven letters. As each is read, ask the class to be making a list of what they tell us to hope for. 2:7; 2:11; 2:17; 2:26-29; 3:5-6; 3:12-13; 3:21-22. **Q:** What does Christ tell Christians to hope for? (Make a list on the board as students share what we hope for.) **Q:** When all of these are taken together, what hope does Christ tell His people about? (Heaven.) **Q:** In each case, the reward is said to be for those who do what? (Overcome.) The Greek word here is *nike*, which means to win the victory by overcoming the obstacles. **Q:** What are some things we should be doing to be sure we are overcomers?

7. **Q:** What are the seven principles we have studied in this lesson and last lesson that come from the seven letters? **Q:** Which of these is going to be the most help to you?

8. In preparation for the next lesson, read Revelation 4-7 and the first half of Lesson 3 in your book.

LESSON 3
CLASS SESSIONS 5 AND 6

CLASS SESSON 5
TEXT: REVELATION 4-7

1. Introduce visitors, sing about Revelation ("Worthy Art Thou" or "Worthy is the Lamb" would be good), and have a prayer for us to exalt Christ in our lives. Answer quiz questions and review the preceding lesson.

2. Open your Bible to Revelation 4. This chapter begins the storyline of Revelation. It is a story told in figures at one level, but the meaning is found as we interpret the figures. So it is like this. (Teacher hold your right hand and forearm in front of you with left hand and forearm underneath. Use this position often to demonstrate that we are dealing a story told with figurative language at one level and that we must look beneath the figures to the meaning at another level.)

3. Use a chalkboard or marker board to draw something like the drawing in chapter 3 to demonstrate the picture John gives of the "stage" on which this drama is played. Let the class help you draw this as they look at the items in Revelation 4.

4. Chapter 5. Q: What does God hold in His hand? Q: Who comes to open it? Q: What do we learn about *when* these events are taking place from the appearance of the Lamb?

5. Chapter 6. Q: What does the Lamb begin to do? Q: What happens when each of the first four seals is broken? Q: Who gives the horsemen their power and authority? Q: It says horsemen (right arm across the body) but what does it mean? (left arm beneath and across the body) It means that God is in control of nations and can make them to rise and fall at His bidding. We cannot comprehend how God allows men free will and at the same time can take what they do and work it into the tapestry of His will.

6.   Q: As the fifth seal is opened, who asks a question? Q: What do they ask? Q: What is God's answer? Revelation 6:9-11 tells us the real question which the book of Revelation is written to answer. So hang on to this question and its answer.

7.   Have someone read Revelation 6:12-17. Using information from chapter 3 in the book, trace these expressions back to their source in the Old Testament. Q: So what do these expressions mean here? (They are indications that God is about to bring the fall of another nation as He did in those passages read from the Old Testament.)

8.   Q: In the interlude between the sixth and seventh seal, what does God want to do for His people? Q: How many does He mark? Q: Who are God's people when this is written? Q: Is the number 144,000 to be taken literally or figuratively?
        Q: Why does God want to put His mark on those who are His people?

9.   Q: Who is seen in heaven serving God in Revelation 7:9-17? Q: How is their condition described? So, if those receiving this book are threatened with martyrdom, this wonderful state awaits them. Q: How is this teaching an encouragement to us?

10.   Assign the students to read Revelation 8-11 for the next class period and to read the last half of Lesson 3 in the book.

TEACHING CLASS SESSION 6
TEXT: REVELATION 8-11

1.   Introduce visitors, give review (oral and written), sing a song about Revelation, and pray for wisdom from God.

CHAPTER 8

2.   Q: After the seventh seal is opened and there is silence for half an hour, who comes on the scene? As each of these angels blows his

trumpet some event takes place. **Q**: Why were trumpets often blown in the Old Testament? **Q**: Who is God wanting to warn at this point in the story? **Q**: How will they respond to this warning? (Read 9:20-21.)

3. The first six trumpets show us how God will warn the persecutor. **Q**: What happens to what when the first four trumpets are blown? **Q**: These four places would make up all what? **Q**: What type of events might these symbolize as warnings?

CHAPTER 9

4. **Q**: What comes when the fifth trumpet is blown? **Q**: Where do they come from? **Q**: What does this place symbolize in Revelation? **Q**: Whom do the locusts afflict and for how long? **Q**: So what do these locusts symbolize in the story?

5. **Q**: What happens and where when the sixth trumpet sounds? **Q**: What is the significance of the Euphrates River here? **Q**: So what message is God giving from the sixth seal?

6. Let's summarize. **Q**: Angels blow trumpets to symbolize what? **Q**: Who is being warned? **Q**: What three basic methods will God use to warn the persecuting Empire to see if it will change its ways? **Q**: What response will the Empire give to these warnings?

CHAPTER 10

7. Now comes an interlude between the sixth and sevenths trumpets. **Q**: Who descends from heaven and what does he do? **Q**: What does he give John and what is John to do with it? This second scroll is the message which John uses to prophesy again in Revelation 12-22.

8. **Q**: What does the temple symbolize? **Q**: What does God promise about it? **Q**: What do the two witnesses represent and what happens to them? **Q**: How long did the assault last on the church and on the witnesses? This length of time represents figuratively the period of the persecution of the Roman Empire which ran from about 90 A.D. to 300 A.D. **Q**: What eventually happens to the witnesses? **Q**: What is the identity of "the great city"? Although the witnesses are killed, they do not stay dead and are taken up to heaven. This symbolizes their victory while the city which opposed them is hit with a great earthquake.

9. When the seventh trumpet blows, we see into heaven. **Q**: What is the mood in heaven at this point? **Q**: Why are they celebrating? And with this celebration because God is now ready to make His move to bring down the persecutor, the curtain closes on Act 1. There is great rejoicing over the fact that God is now going to make His move against the persecutor.

10. **Q**: How can we use this part of the story to help us be faithful?

11. Assign the reading of Revelation 12-14 for next time, along with the first half of Lesson 4 in the book.

LESSON 4
CLASS SESSIONS 7 AND 8

TEACHING CLASS SESSION 7
TEXT: REVELATION 12-15

1. Introduce visitors, sing about Revelation, pray, and review with test answers.

2. Q: How did the last lesson close? (With joy in heaven because of the announcement that God was ready to destroy the one who has been destroying.)

3. With the beginning of chapter 12, we start Act 2 of the story of Revelation. The first act was told through the opening of the first scroll. In chapter 10, John was given a second scroll and told to prophesy again. Since chapter 12 is after the seventh trumpet, last event of the first scroll, this would appear to mark the beginning of John's use of the second scroll.

4. Q: Who is pictured as chapter 12 begins and how is she described? (Write the descriptive statements of the woman on the board. Collect these descriptions as you go through chapter 12 and then try to identify the woman.) Q: What does the woman do? Q: Who is the child? Q: Who seeks to destroy the child? Q: Who is the dragon? Q: How is the child protected? So Satan loses round 1.

5. Next there is war in heaven. Q: Who is fighting? Q: Who wins? Q: What is the result of this war? It would seem, then, that Satan was trying to stop Christ from taking His place as savior because when Satan loses this fight and is cast out, those cleansed by the blood of Christ have their sins forgiven and Satan can no longer accuse them of wrongdoing. So Satan loses round 2.

6. Next, Satan seeks to harm the woman. Q: How does God protect her? (Add this to your list about the woman.) So Satan loses round 3.

7.   Satan now makes another move. He will attack the "offspring" of the woman. **Q**: Who are these children of the woman? (Add this to your list about the woman.) Before we study this fourth attack, let's stop and identify the woman.

Review the qualities of the woman you have listed. **Q**: Which of these would fit Mary who gave birth to Jesus? She could not qualify for most of these. **Q**: Which of these would fit the Jewish nation? That nation could not qualify for most of these. Christians surely, for example, would not be thought of as the children of the Jewish nation when, as a whole, that nation opposed Christianity. **Q**: Which of these qualities would fit the church? The church is not the mother of Christ nor are Christians the offspring of the church. They are the church. Here is another possibility—the eternal plan of God. Romans 8:28, for example, speaks of those called "according to His purpose." **Q**: How well would taking the woman as God's eternal plan fit the characteristics? The plan gave birth to Christ. Satan tried to stop the plan. The plan also gave birth to Christians. So the woman would seem to represent "God's eternal plan."

8.   To carry out his war against the church, Satan brings up two beasts. From looking at 13:1-8 and 17:9-10, let's list the characteristics of the beast. (Review from Lesson 1.) **Q**: To what entity would these point? Now let's list the characteristics of the second beast. (Review from Lesson 1.) **Q**: To what entity would these point?

9.   Satan's fourth attack is now clear. He wants to wipe out the church through persecution. He wants to use the most powerful force on earth to do that. **Q**: What is the most powerful force on earth at that time? But the Roman Empire allows many different religions. Why would they want to destroy the church? That is the role of the second beast—emperor worship. Satan will put Christians in a dilemma—either deny your faith in Christ by worshipping the emperor or be killed. Either way, Satan would

seem to win. What he had not counted on, however, is that the way Christians would die for Christ attracted others who wanted to find out what they had that was so good it was worth dying for. So as Satan killed many, others were attracted and he did not succeed in eradicating the church.

10. By the time we come to the end of chapter 13, the period of intense persecution, led by the Roman Empire and the Cult of Emperor Worship, is over. The "42 months" is done.

11. **Q**: In chapter 14, who is now seen in heaven? **Q**: How did they get from being on earth (chapter 7) to now being in heaven? Now they are in heaven following the Lamb wherever He goes. **Q**: What announcement comes in verse 9? The fall of the persecutor is now announced and predicted. **Q**: What did we study earlier that parallels this? (Revelation 11:15b-18.)

12. **Q**: In chapter 15, when John looks into heaven, what group does he see? **Q**: Did the beast kill them? **Q**: Who won? So dying is not the worst thing that can happen to us. For Christians that only brings the time of victory. We need to see death in this light. **Q**: How can we learn to take this view of death and help others to do the same?

13. For next time, read Revelation 15-19 and the last half of Lesson 4, and study for the quiz.

TEACHING CLASS SESSION 8
TEXT: REVELATION 16-19

1. Introduce visitors, pray, sing about Revelation, give test answers and review.

2. **Q**: What do seven angels have and what will they do with them? Against whom will the plagues be directed? **Q**: When did God, at an earlier time, pour out plagues on a nation in retribution for their persecuting His people?

3.   Q: On what and on whom does the first angel pour out his bowl?
        Q: On what does the second angel pour out his bowl? Q: On
        what and does an angel pour out the third bowl and who is
        affected in particular? Q: On what does the fourth angel pour out
        his bowl? Q: How do those affected respond? Q: On what is the
        fifth bowl poured out and what is its effect? (Makes the throne
        of the beast to be dark. Immorality eventually will bring down
        any kingdom.) Q: On what does the sixth angel pour out his
        bowl and why? Q: What major event, then, is symbolized by the
        six bowls and what means will God use to achieve this?

4.   Between the sixth and seventh bowls, there is an interlude. Q:
        During this time, who has a meeting to decide what to do? Q:
        What do they do? Q: Where do they tell their vassal kings to
        gather? Q: What significance does that place have? Q: Does this
        effort to resist God's plan for destroying the Roman Empire
        bring any delay in the outcome? Q: What happens when the sev-
        enth angel pours out his bowl? The fall of the Roman Empire
        brings to an end the major message of Revelation. The next three
        chapters elaborate on that event with more details but chapter 19
        will end at the same point in time as does chapter 16.

5.   Q: What new character is introduced in chapter 17? Q: From
        verses 1-6 and 15-18, what are the qualities of this woman?
        (Write them on the board.) Q: Since verse 18 says the woman is
        "the great city," we must ask what city can fit all the qualifica-
        tions given here.

6.   In chapter 18, we learn of the consequences of resisting what
        God has said to do. The city, with the code name of Babylon and
        represented by the prostitute, is shown with the troubles of its
        fall. Q: What groups of people are sad with her fall?

7.   Have someone read Revelation 19:1-3. Q: Why is there rejoicing
        in heaven? Q: How does this connect with Revelation 6:10?
        (Judge and avenge our blood.)

8. **Q**: What characteristics identify the rider on the white horse? **Q**: Who follows him? **Q**: Against whom does He come? **Q**: What does He do with them?

9. So chapters 17-19 end with the fall of the beast just as did chapter 16. These three chapters provide more details than were given in Revelation 16:17-20. **Q**: Of the four forces for evil given in Revelation, which have now gone down to defeat? **Q**: Which one is left?

10. **Q**: When are some times we would benefit from remembering that God is really the one in control and can turn apparent setbacks into victory?

11. Chapter 20 will deal with what happens next to the dragon (Satan). For next time, prepare for the quiz and read Revelation 20 and the first half of Lesson 5.

LESSON 5
CLASS SESSIONS 9 AND 10

TEACHING CLASS SESSON 9
TEXT: REVELATION 20:1-6

1. Introduce visitors, sing a Revelation song, prayer, check quiz answers.

2. Today our study is about the thousand-year period in Revelation 20. This is one of the most controversial passages in the Bible and so it is very important that we have the view of it Christ intended when He sent this message to the seven churches of Asia.

3. Q: What happened at the close of chapter 19? Q: Of the four main evil characters in the book of Revelation, who is left as chapter 20 begins?

4. The first three verses of the chapter tell of the binding of Satan for a thousand years. Read Revelation 20:1-3. Q: What picture is given in these three verses of the binding of Satan? Q: Has Satan always been bound? Limited? Q: What are some of the other occasions in the Bible when Satan was limited or bound? Q: Are all of these parallel? Q: In what way is Satan said to be limited in this case? Q: What had he been doing in the previous part of Revelation? So this limiting says he will not be permitted to do again what he had just done—use a world-wide empire to try to persecute the church out of existence.

5. Read Revelation 20:4-6. There was a thousand-year binding and now there will be a thousand-year reigning. We will study this thousand-year reign by asking four questions about it.

6. Question 1—Who reigns? Q: How does the text describe those who reign with Christ? Q: What condition are these in when they reign? (Souls.) Q: Where have we seen these souls before in the book of Revelation? The answer to the "who reigns" question then is *the souls of the martyrs of the Roman persecution.*

7.	Question 2—Why do they reign? While the text does not direct-ly answer this question, the context will. **Q**: What event marked the end of chapter 19 and thus the beginning point of chapter 20? **Q**: What do we do when we have won a victory over our enemy? **Q**: So what would it mean to those Christians persecuted in the early centuries to say that after their martyrdom and after the fall of their persecutor they will reign with Christ? As part of the symbolic story in Revelation, then, chapter 20 tells that when their enemy falls, the souls of the martyrs will enjoy *a great and long victory celebration.*

8.	Question 3—Where will they reign? The pre-millennial theory suggests that this reign is on earth. What does the passage say? **Q**: Does the text say directly where the reign will be? Let's look to some other indicators. **Q**: In what realm do "souls" without bodies exist? **Q**: Where have these souls been seen before? **Q**: Where has Christ been seen before? **Q**: Where have thrones been seen before? **Q**: Where, then, would we expect this reign to be? The best answer to the "where question," then, is that this reign takes place *in the spirit realm which we may call heaven.*

9.	Question 4—When will they reign? **Q**: What event marks the beginning of the thousand years? **Q**: What event is described in verses 11-15 of chapter 20? **Q**: How long a time is there between the end of the thousand years and the coming of the judgment? We will study the "little time" in our next lesson, but for now we can note that only a short time—days, weeks, months, maybe a few years—stands between the end of the thousand years and the end of time. We may, then, answer the "when question" by saying that the thousand years *begins at the fall of Rome about 475 A.D. and ends shortly before the end of time.*

10.	From the text within its context, then, we understand the thou-sand-year reign. Like most everything else in Revelation, it is symbolic. Says thousand-year reign. What does it mean? This picture is to tell those about to be persecuted by the Roman

Empire that if they are martyred for the cause of Christ, they have something wonderful to look forward to. They will some-day celebrate with Christ their faithfulness and the great victory this made possible because the church survives and the Roman Emperor and Cult of Emperor Worship have gone down to defeat. And for a long time, they will experience the joy of that victory. The intent of this passage is certainly not to predict a thousand-year reign of Christ on earth.

11. Q: What are victories over which we should be rejoicing?

12. Remind of the test next time and assign the reading of Revelation 20:7-15 and the last half of Lesson 5.

TEACHING CLASS SESSION 10
TEXT: REVELATION 20:7-15

1. Welcome visitors, sing a song about Revelation, pray, and review by checking answers to the quiz.

2. From the last lesson a couple of questions to get us started. Q: What are the two major things Revelation 20 says will happen for a thousand years? Q: What message do we get from the bind-ing of Satan? Q: What message do we get from the thousand year reign with Christ?

3. The second section of Revelation 20 is found in verses 7-10. Let's read those. Q: How long is this period said to be? Q: What events take place in this "little time"? Q: How are God's people described in these verses? Q: Are these people said to be harmed in any way? Q: Should we take this to mean that there will be a great persecution of Christians just before the end of the world? Q: What does God do to Satan at the end of this short time? Q: What is the meaning of being thrown into the Lake of Fire?

4. The third section of Revelation 20 is found in verses 11-15—a description of the final judgment. Read these verses. Q: Who

will appear before the judgment throne of God? **Q**: What will be the standard for this final judgment? **Q**: What group of people will go away approved from this judgment? Read some verses about the book of life: Exodus 32:33; Luke 10:20; Philippians 4:3; Revelation 3:5; Revelation 20:15; Revelation 21:27. **Q**: What conclusions can we draw from these verses about the book of Life? **Q**: What are the possible conditions one might be in relative to the book of life? **Q**: What are the destinations of the two groups at this judgment? **Q**: Can one know if he/she is written in the book of life?

5. This is a good time for all of us to ask if we are written in the book of life.

6. Assignment for next time is to prepare for the quiz, read chapters 21 and 22 of Revelation, and read the first half of Lesson 6.

LESSON 6
CLASS SESSIONS 11 AND 12

TEACHING CLASS SESSON 11
TEXT: REVELATION 21-22

1.   Introduce visitors, sing a song connected with Revelation, pray, provide answers to the quiz.

2.   To get the context for this lesson, we must look back to the Revelation 20:11-15. **Q**: From that judgment, what are the two destinies to which people are sent? **Q**: What determines to which destiny one is sent? **Q**: How can one be assured that he/she is written in the book of life? **Q**: How is the destiny of those not written in the book of life pictured?

3.   Revelation 21 and 22 picture the destiny of those who are written in the book of life. We will study this today and then in our last lesson, we will review our study of the book of Revelation. Read Revelation 21:1-4. **Q**: What do these verses emphasize as they describe the New Jerusalem? (The close relationship between God and His people.) We are going to read the verses describing the New Jerusalem and will write on the board the characteristics as we talk about the verses. Read Revelation 21:11-18. **Q**: How do these verses portray what the city looks like from the outside? Read Revelation 21:22-22:5. **Q**: What do these verses say the city is like on the inside?

4.   Since this, like other things in Revelation, uses symbolic terms, let's discuss what overall conception Christ wants us to get from this picture of heavenly existence. Heaven here is pictured as a perfect place. I am going to suggest some ways in which it is perfect and let you tell the descriptions that would show that quality. Heaven will give *perfect protection*. **Q**: What descriptions would suggest this protection the city offers? Heaven will offer *perfect fellowship*. **Q**: What descriptions would suggest the fellow-

ship the city offers? Heaven will offer *perfect provisions*. **Q**: What descriptions would suggest the provisions the city offers? The city offers *perfect joy*. **Q**: What descriptions would suggest the perfect joy the city offers?

5.   From the following verses we can get Christ's advice on how to be included in heaven. We'll read the verse and then ask you to summarize the advice. Revelation 22:14. **Q**: What does Christ advise us to do? Revelation 22:15. **Q**: What does Christ advise us not to do? Revelation 22:17. **Q**: What would these verses teach us about going to heaven?

6.   The assignment for next time is to prepare for the quiz. We will spend the next class session reviewing Revelation and making some applications to ourselves.

TEACHING CLASS SESSION 12
REVIEW OF THE BOOK OF REVELATION

1.   Introduce visitors, sing about heaven as pictured in Revelation, pray for all of us to enjoy heaven together, give the answers for the quiz.

2.   In this lesson we will summarize what we have been studying in the book of Revelation. (Teacher—be sure to close the lesson with Nos. 5 and 6 even if you do not get to all the others. If you have lesson 13 available, these questions could easily be spread over two periods.) **Q**: What was the primary message of the book Christ wanted the Christians of the late first century and next two centuries to get? **Q**: What does the book reveal that Satan's strategy was? **Q**: What lesson would Christ want us to get from this message?

3.   In Christ's letters to the seven churches, He gave lots of advice about what He wanted Christians and churches to be like. **Q**: What advice from chapters 2 and 3 do you think would be especially helpful for us?

4.   The church of the early centuries faced dangers from without and within. **Q**: What do you think are some of the dangers the church faces today?

5.   **Q**: How can this study of Revelation help us in being more evangelistic?

6.   The book of Revelation is a book of hope. **Q**: What message of hope do you believe Christ would have us get from this book today?